And Then I Met This Woman

Previously Married Women's Journeys
into Lesbian Relationships

Barbee J. Cassingham, M.A.
Sally M. O'Neil, Ph.D.

Published by

Mother Courage Press
1667 Douglas Avenue
Racine, WI 53404

Library of Congress catalog card number 93-77708
ISBN 0-941300-25-0

Mother Courage Press
1667 Douglas Avenue
Racine, WI 53404-2721

Dedication

This book is dedicated to these
women who opened their lives to us.

Acknowledgments

We wish to express our deep appreciation to
Linda Vogt for her expert assistance with format,
title and editing. Our appreciation also goes to
Leslie Woods for her editing work. Both of these
women reviewed the manuscript many times and
gave much encouragement and support.

Much appreciation to Betty who arranged the
interviews in Texas.

Introduction

These are the remarkable stories of women whose lives have been transformed by intimacy with another woman. Many had lived a very traditional, heterosexual life up until that point—whenever it was—and made a conscious decision to change.

The women in these stories are mostly middle class and represent diverse occupations: an oncology nurse, a minister, an English professor, a topless-dancer-turned-beautician, teachers, a computer programmer, a florist, counselors, a nurse anesthetist. Many are highly educated, six with master's degrees, and four with Ph.D.s. They range in age from 27 to 65. These interviews were done in Texas, Arizona and the Pacific Northwest.

We chose to publish as many stories as possible rather than only a few in depth. We wanted to show the diversity as well as the commonalities of these women's experience. In addition, we chose not to present an analysis of these interviews but, rather to let the women speak for themselves.

Of the 36 women who tell their stories here, not one regrets her decision to change her sexuality—and her life. For many, making the transition from heterosexual wifehood to lesbianism was like "coming home," and they wouldn't even consider going back.

We were impressed with each woman's willingness and openness in telling her story. These women knew the book's purpose, and they wanted to share what they learned in order to help someone else who might be struggling through conflict and chaos in discovering an attraction to another woman.

These stories may show women that if they decide to act on their feelings for other women, they won't fall into a pit of perverts and strange people. The women in these pages, like women in your life, are good people—lesbians who lead satisfying lives!

The biggest surprise for us in doing these interviews was to discover just how easily some of the women made these transitions even after as many as 20 years of traditional, married, heterosexually-identified lives. Very few went to a counselor; they just simply moved into their new way of being.

The value of this work, as we see it, is the discovery that we are experiencing a change in our society. We are in a time when women are more able to realize they can have a choice in their love relationships. They are finding the power to follow their hearts, and they are more able to accept lesbianism for themselves.

In offering this book, we do not want readers to think that we are suggesting that lesbianism, in and of itself, is a utopia. In fact, lesbian relationships, as any other, can be difficult. We are not advocating lesbianism as a choice for every woman. Instead, we are offering the stories of these 36 women who have been in traditional marriages and have instead chosen life with another woman. These women feel their lives are vastly improved by having made that choice; with a woman, finally they were home.

Many of the women interviewed told us that when they were wondering what to do with their feelings for women and with their lives, they had wished there had been a book like this; they wanted more information. We offer these stories to serve that purpose.

We are touched that these women told us about their lives and their dreams. It is our hope that their dreams are fulfilled.

Barbee Cassingham
Sally O'Neil

Contents

Janet

Coming to terms with being a lesbian took a long time. All
the rules for social interaction, as I knew them,
were out the window.

Janet is 41. She was born in San Francisco. She has had four major
fields of employment in which she educated herself. She is currently
working as a licensed massage therapist.

"I was married in March of 1967. I was young—16—and
pregnant.

"I married a man whose mother opposed the marriage. She
was very high up in the Selective Service at that time, and her
response was to see that he was drafted! He was shipped out
pretty quickly to Vietnam.

"He came back in 1969 and was in pretty bad shape. He
hadn't actually done combat, but he had been traumatized by
being over there. We were ill-matched to begin with and, in the
interval, I had grown in a different direction. We stayed
together for another year because I had a commitment to
helping him adjust back into the world from where he had
been. I did that and then we separated.

"I was the one who filed for divorce. We would probably
have stayed together longer, but he was gambling a lot at that
time and also womanizing. There were limits to what I would
endure. So, I ended that marriage; that was in 1970.

"After that, I entered a long-term relationship with my
employer, who was a male veterinarian. We were romantically
involved for sometime, and then we started living together in
1971. We stayed together until I got in touch with my sexual
preference in 1977.

"For me, it was the lack of a fulfilling sexual relationship
that ended it. We were in counseling at that time, and I was just
really waking up. Looking back now, I feel that I was coming

1

out of a fog. I had been reacting to things all of my life. I began becoming more pro-active. I was a late bloomer. I had never had an orgasm with him or with any man. I discovered that I really was a lesbian—and that's what ended the relationship.

"I was teaching photography at that time and I had a friendship with a number of people involved with the local camera store. The strongest friendship was with a woman there. The time with her was quality time. We did a lot of things together and one night she suggested that we all go into San Francisco for the evening. There was a police officer and his wife and the two of us. So we went—and we ended up at Peg's Place, which is a lesbian bar.

"I hadn't the foggiest idea what I had landed in. I was really shocked—and totally unprepared. I had no idea this was where we were going to go. I was trying to be cool, and cope, and be appropriate. The next thing I knew, I was on the dance floor dancing with my friend, Karen!

"She seduced me that night, and it wasn't terribly difficult. We spent almost the entire night together. We ended up going home before dawn. That just turned my whole world upside down and was really hard for me. I had an incredible amount of internalized homophobia. I hadn't even come into my feminism yet. I was very male-identified. I was a good wife, a good partner, coming from the '50's . . . Betty Crocker—the whole thing. I could hardly say 'lesbian' without gagging.

"Coming to terms with being a lesbian took a long time. All the rules for social interaction, as I knew them, were out the window. It was all very confusing.

"I was now in a new culture, and within that, more subcultures. At Peg's, I met women who ironed their white shirts on Friday night. They had their black slacks, and their high collars, and they would go out just so. They had a certain way about them that I just loved to watch, and they'd play pool and do all these things. That's not my identity.

"Now I really enjoy those women, but that is a different subculture from my own. At the time, I had no idea. I thought that that was what I was going to be. The tough women at the bar . . . I felt like I was running a gauntlet when I went in there. I felt the lack of any guidelines for how to negotiate all this.

"My friend was amused more than anything else. She wasn't terribly helpful in understanding all this. She was incredibly powerful in my life at that time, but she really wasn't there to help.

"There was a rap group I'd heard about in the neighborhood and I went—but the first time I went, I couldn't even go in. I drove up and I sat in front, and I couldn't get out of the car. Then I left.

"The next time I went, I almost made it to the door. Then someone came along and sort of swept me in. That was really the beginning of being helped. There was a very diverse group in the room and I got a sense of different possibilities. There were lots of different bars in Marin and I found where I was comfortable.

"This first woman and I had a very wonderful, hot, passionate affair, which ended the relationship with the man I had been with. He and I continued to work together and have remained friends. He took it pretty well, all things considered. I did tell him what was going on. His response was to become involved with a succession of very young, very pretty women. That was fine.

"My woman friend and I carried on for quite a while. Then I found out that her roommate was not really her roommate but was really a woman that she had a committed relationship with. I felt very betrayed and hurt and angry. She hadn't told me that. It was months before she told me. We carried on after that but I felt uncomfortable. That wasn't what I wanted.

"Even after that when I would have a photography show, she would come and, for me, the whole room would stop and there would be nothing but her. She had that much of a hold over me. I eventually said that I couldn't continue doing that.

"There were many subsequent relationships with women. I got a sense of what dating was and I wouldn't want to do that again. Dating is difficult. I eventually dated a number of Karin's ex-lovers and we discovered that all we had to talk about was Karin!

3

"I am currently in a relationship and Hannah and I will soon be together seven years. It's going wonderfully. I met her at my job. We became friends those first six months. I was in two other relationships during that time; then Hannah and I got together. We had gone down to a poetry reading by Adriene Rich and during the trip down and back it became clear to me that I wanted to be with her. So now it's seven years, and it gets better and deeper—and it's wonderful.

"Prior to this move, I've always been out. But there is a huge fundamentalist Christian community where I live now. So, I'm out to only some of the community. I'm out to my immediate friends, and to women's groups in the area. I helped organize the lesbian community here.

"My father is dead. He died two years after I came out. My mother is alive and living in California. When I first came out to them it was O.K.; they weren't particularly upset. But after my Dad died, my mother had a fit about me being a lesbian. She said she was containing her feelings because of my dad's health. We didn't talk for a few years. Finally, now, she accepts my lifestyle, although she doesn't agree with it.

"I am out to my brother and sister. My sister fluctuates between being supportive and not but mostly, she is accepting. My brother is fine about it.

"I did have a child from my marriage, but we gave him up for adoption at birth. I just found him this last spring. It's a pretty powerful thing in my life. He is now 24, and he is pretty amazing. He was raised in Tennessee. He's been raised to be pretty working class and very Southern—a good ol' boy. He's very bigoted, very racist. But, I came out to him in the second conversation we had and he has been extremely accepting. We call every so often. He's not into writing. He considers Hannah his stepmother, and considers her family. It really is amazing. Hannah and I are planning on having a child, and he is totally involved in that. Hannah will be the biological mother.

"It's very difficult not being out to everyone. I'm accustomed to being out and, since moving to this rural area, it's been very difficult. I don't like hiding; I don't like the power that one gives away. I don't like not being able to be myself and having to be on guard all the time.

"Five or so years from now, I don't think my life will be very different. I've made a decision to put serious roots down here. I've invested a lot of time and energy in starting my massage practice here. I intend to continue that. I'm sure my partner and I will grow old together.

"My advice for women who are beginning to feel they might be a lesbian is to find a support group. Join any local lesbian center. It would be ideal if you could find a coming-out group. I also think subscribing to lesbian publications helps. My pick would be the *Lesbian Connection* because it speaks from the heart.

"I would like to tell other women that I know how hard it is to make that change. At least it was for me. I think it helps to have a feminist orientation to begin with. If I had been female-identified, I wouldn't have bought into so many of the male ideas.

"You should just be kind to yourself. You should believe what your gut and heart say. I believed what my clit said and went with that—even when the rational stuff was at odds with what I was feeling.

"You should know that if it's right for you, you'll be able to move through the difficulties."

Julia

I consider myself out, but it took 60 years!

Julia is 65. She was born in Chicago, Illinois. She attended two years of community college.

"I was married in 1945 and it lasted for 34 years. For 20 of those 34 years I had a relationship with a woman. That is the crux of it!

"I met this other married woman through the Junior League. After about seven years, my husband was transferred to Philadelphia. By this time, of course, she and I were very involved and we spent the next 13 years with her coming to Philadelphia and me spending the summers with her in Chicago. My children would always be at camp each summer, and she didn't have any kids.

"In those 13 years we wrote every day and we called once a week. Looking back, I think we were living a fantasy. When we finally did get together, it busted up. The sexual part of the relationship sort of waned and that may have been part of the problem. We lost it from all of the stress we were under and there was a lot of homophobia in both of us. And, also, she had a wandering eye and had affairs with women which I closed my eyes to. But I was, in reality, very ambivalent.

"Six weeks after I called it quits, she was in another affair. In order to win her back, I got a divorce. It was a very hard thing for me to do. You see, I married a peach of a guy. He just thought I was swell. He was easy. He would have stuck with me—he didn't care what I did. I think he knew all along what was going on. He wanted peace at any price and he didn't want the stigma of divorce and he did not want to be abandoned. He would have hung in there, but it was my guilt that was killing me.

"So, I finally got a divorce to be with my friend. Then, when that didn't work, I felt that I had sacrificed a tremendous amount. In essence, I was saying to her, 'Look what I have given up for you. Now it is your turn to take care of me.' This was not owning my part because I really wanted to be with her. Also, I didn't take the responsibility to make that relationship go.

"As a result of the breakup, I've had a lot of therapy to determine what was going on with me. As I look back, I think it was that I couldn't handle the closeness. She wasn't perfect, but she was pretty great.

"It has been a terrible three years. I have never experienced being abandoned before. She was everything to me, and I had a lot of pain. But, I'm feeling much better. I'm wiser. I'm smarter. I'm out of my fantasy world. I had a lot to learn about being on my own. It's taken me a long time to let go of that relationship. I'm being honest with you because you are writing a book that might help other people.

"I have three daughters. My oldest is very supportive of me and my lifestyle. You see, I spent my life hiding it. My oldest daughter said she knew there were secrets in the house and she did not want any secrets. She, too, has three daughters and she didn't want her daughters to grow up with these secrets. So here I was—the most homophobic individual and I was placed in a spot. So, after the split-up, I told all my daughters. My middle daughter will not discuss it, and she and I have a lousy relationship. My youngest daughter doesn't say much about it. We don't discuss it, but she and I get along fine.

"My oldest daughter asked me to tell my grandchildren. It was the most difficult thing to do, but it worked out fine. They say to others, 'What's the matter with a gay person?' It's neat. I think, now, they just look at me as Grandma. My ex-husband moved to Florida and remarried a few years ago. I told him, too. Now he thinks he is better than I am and is stuffy as can be. I see him about every other year when he comes to see the children and we get along fine.

"When the break-up happened, I thought, 'Now that's all behind me. I'll go back to the straight world.' I'm a bridge player, and I have the Baptist Church. Between the church and my bridge, I thought I would meet people. I planned to close the door on the gay world. Well, it was very lonely. Life was pretty dull and pretty awful. I do have some church members that I still see and I still play bridge, but, I find myself doing it less and less. I am much happier being who I really am, and being part of a lesbian group. I consider myself out, but it took about sixty years!

"After this breakup, I just climbed into the wine bottle—night after night. Then I went to a treatment center. They told me they thought I was alcoholic and that I ought to say off booze. So I joined AA and that has been very positive for me. I go to both gay and straight meetings. I made friends through AA and they are people I do things with. I hope that some meaningful person comes into my life.

"To be honest, I think everybody looks for a companion. I think I could be responsible in a relationship now. I was so ambivalent before. I was torn between the woman and the tapes of my mother in my head that said I should be married. I knew in my heart of hearts what I really wanted. I was so pulled.

"For the woman who is thinking about changing I would say, 'Stop torturing yourself.' I tried to go back to the straight world and it didn't work. I lost my relationship because I was so full of ambivalence. Make up your mind and go one way or the other—but I'd suggest going the gay route. We all know people who deny their lesbianism and are miserable. I'm learning to enjoy people and to not be so afraid of life."

Lauren

I consider Bonnie to be someone I happened to meet and fall in love with, and want to share my life with. But I don't necessarily consider myself a lesbian.

Lauren is 40. She was born in Salem, Oregon. She has a B.S. in elementary education and teaches third grade.

"I was married in 1971, and it lasted for six years. I met my husband in college in California where we were in the same music classes. I knew him for about a year and though we didn't plan to get married, I got pregnant. It was a surprise to both of us. I came to Oregon to go to school and was registered and everything, and then found out I was pregnant. I went back to Palm Springs and we got married in November of that year.

"I knew when we were getting married that I shouldn't because I didn't love him. His parents were very rich, and they bought us a house, two cars and put $5,000 into a checking account.

"Meanwhile, my mother wanted me to get an abortion. But every time I was supposed to sign something, I kept crying. My doctor thought that was a sign I really didn't want to have an abortion, and he was right. I knew that this would be the only child I would ever have, and I knew she would be a girl, and I even knew on what day she would be born.

"The night I brought the baby home, Al was in college and he was going to have a test the next day, so he spent that night with his parents. He said it was too noisy to be around me and the baby. It made me feel awful and I felt very deserted. He didn't know how to be a husband. We were both 20.

"Our daughter will be 20 this year. While I was married, I put myself through school. I was able to apply for grants on my own. I didn't own anything that we had.

"Through most of our marriage, we were good friends; we're still good friends now. We finally got divorced because I was just too unhappy. I didn't want to be married anymore. I didn't want to live with him anymore.

"I have never found the term 'lesbian' comfortable, but I know by other people's descriptions that that's what I would be. It is important for me to be thought of as a heterosexual because I am a teacher. I consider Bonnie to be someone I happened to meet and fall in love with—and want to share my life with. But I don't necessarily consider myself a lesbian.

"I met her at my friend Kate's when I went to visit. Bonnie was there all the time and I could hardly talk to Kate alone. It turned out that they were in a relationship.

"During this time in my life, I was very unaware of my own sexuality. When I found out a woman could have an orgasm, I went immediately to Kate and told her. I thought she couldn't possibly know that, and she was very kind and listened. I had taken a class called Preorgasmic Women and had started reading books about women having relationships with each other. I felt very compelled to teach Bonnie and Kate about these experiences that they could have!

"I thought the home they created together was so cozy and warm. It didn't occur to me that this could be a way I could live. As Bonnie and I became closer, Kate began a relationship with another woman, and she moved in there, too. Before long I moved in with them and the four of us lived together for a year. Then Kate and her friend split up and Kate moved to Portland to be closer to her job, and Bonnie and I have been together ever since.

"When I was first separated and moved out, Al was determined that Kate was the reason we split up. He came to pick up our daughter one day at my apartment. I wasn't home and he went upstairs and got my journal where I had hidden it. I had written a lot about dreams and about Kate because she was someone I could talk to. He was going to take me to court for custody of our daughter. He was looking for evidence that I was an unfit mother. That was a big deal and a lot of trust I had with Al was destroyed at that time. The journal got in the hands of lawyers and finally the agreement was that he would pay no more child support. I think today he still thinks that Kate is the cause of our divorce.

"After I was divorced, I was a counselor in a teen parent program. I was the person the teens would come to when they first found out they were pregnant, and I would help them with their options. After that, I got a job as a teacher and have been a teacher ever since.

"When I started living with Bonnie it was really easy. I felt very open and it was much more calming to change into this life. It was everything I ever thought living with a person should be. I have not had other relationships with other women. I was never in counseling for my change in sexual orientation. I have now known Bonnie for 21 years, and we've been together since 1978.

"I am not out to anyone except a few close lesbian friends. I have told my daughter that some people would call the relationship Bonnie and I have 'lesbian' or 'homosexual', but that I don't consider that to be the case. That's honest.

"My daughter lived with us and went to school, so that added a whole different component to the relationship. Now, I think that she thinks that Bonnie and I are the very best of friends, and that we would do anything for each other.

"It is not hard to maintain my secrecy. We are not demonstrative in public. My daughter doesn't live with us anymore, but she feels very free about popping into the school where Bonnie works at anytime and seeing her.

"My mother is living and my father has been dead for 17 years. I'm a survivor of incest from my father. I've just remembered this in the past few years. It's a source of fear to remember those times. I've decided to tell my mom because my mom was there. I don't know whether she remembers it.

"My mom doesn't like Bonnie much. She feels that my alliance to family has changed to Bonnie's family. A lot of that is true because my relationship with my mother is very awkward. Last year I finally asked her if she liked me, and she said that she loved me but she never liked me as a child and as a teenager, and that she feels uncomfortable around me now.

11

"My brother's an alcoholic and we went through a whole intervention program to get him into treatment. When he came out, he went right back into drinking again. My mom supplies him with his liquor. That situation is one of the saddest things in my life.

"I have had some health problems. I have panic attacks and I can't control them. I can't tell when they're going to happen. I know that they come from suppressed feelings about Dad.

"My health is getting better. For awhile it was very poor and I was disabled for two-and-a-half years. During that time, I was raped when a man broke into my house. He wore a ski mask, but I think I know who he is. I have a lot of back pain, still, from that. I see a counselor once a week, I take medication, and I breathe correctly so I won't hyperventilate. It's an ongoing process.

"Before my rape, Bonnie and I used to go hiking and skiing. Now, for fun, I watch TV, read and go to movies. I don't like to be left alone. I have a lot of fun teaching, traveling and seeing friends. As I look into the future, I plan to still be teaching. I'd like to live out in the country and have a horse. I'd like a garden—to get back the earth awareness that I used to have.

"My advice for women who are thinking of changing their sexual orientation is if they think they are lesbian, they probably are. There are lots of things at stake when you are in a marriage with children. A person has to be happy with herself and where she is or it doesn't matter if you have kids or anything. I would advise her to talk to a counselor . . . one who is neutral about sexuality."

Barbara

I knew at seven that I wanted nothing to do with men.

Barbara is 60. She was born in Lake Charles, Louisiana. She has a M.A.
in English, and teaches at a university.

"I was married in 1951 because it was the thing that was
expected. All my friends were getting married and everybody
was looking at me. I wasn't in love, but he was a nice fellow
from a nice family, and I was a nice girl from a nice family, and
everybody thought we were just perfect. We were married 11
years and had two boys during that time. One is now 38 and the
other is 33.

"I was an Army wife during the Korean situation. I got
pregnant within the first year and my family wanted me to
come home as they thought they could do more for me. John,
meanwhile, was accepted into officer's candidate school. The
marriage could have been fine, but I wasn't in love with him
and I drank a lot.

"I tried to conform to the Army's way of doing things and
I was too good at that. He hung in and I think he loved me. I
tried my hardest to make him think that I loved him. Then we
were sent to Japan and I was pregnant again. Next we went
Okinawa. The men were busy and the wives played cards and
such. I was most unhappy. I didn't participate too well as an
Army wife.

"I made a real grand mess of the whole marriage during
those three years on that island. When we got back to the States,
I think both of us knew that the marriage was over. When he
came to get me and the kids for the next move, I just said, 'I'm
sorry. I have had it.' I could not pretend any longer.

"I look back now and I think I was pretty brave. Many of my
friends are still in marriages they hate. They are still there
because they have a nice home in a good area and all that. My
father and my mother had been divorced for many years, and

13

my father lived in Detroit, so I decided to go there. But, it was too damned cold in Detroit! I don't know . . . there was something wrong with me. I was just trying to find me. I got divorced while I was there and, then, I couldn't stay there either. So, I came back to Houston. My kids were here with my mother.

"The first person I met was a friend of my mother's. She was a female doctor. We took one look at each other and that was it. The problem was that everybody in Houston knew that she was gay. My mother and everybody else knew. It was kind of the talk of Houston. I was disgracing the family by going with this woman. That was 1962.

"This doctor and I were together for quite a while and my mother wanted to die. She knew, in spite of the doctor's reputation, I wasn't like that. The doctor was gay but I wasn't, according to my mother. The doctor and my mother were friends and she would come over to visit. My mother noticed that we were going out an awful lot. This just killed my mother. It became such a big deal to everybody that we just decided to forget it. Except we couldn't forget it. We would just sneak off and see each other from time to time. That was the first time I had had a lesbian experience.

"I knew at seven that I wanted nothing to do with men. I just knew. I didn't know what to call myself except 'tomboy.' With the doctor I found a release at last. The weight of the world just fell off my shoulders. We didn't live together, we just saw each other. Actually everything was going pretty well and one day I had to do something and she told me to take her car. Black Houston at that time was very close knit. Everybody knew everything. Here's Barbara in the doctor's car. The people weren't as dumb as we thought. We were together about two years, but there was so much pressure I was just about to go out of my mind. I had to leave her. We both decided we just couldn't do it.

"My mother found a psychiatrist for me. I talked to him until I got tired of him. I told my mother she was wasting her money because he was telling me, 'Well, you have a mother complex and you're not really a gay.' I listened to that and he was charging about $50 dollars an hour—in those days that was a lot of money.

"My current partner, Sue, and I just celebrated our twenty-first anniversary. When I first went to work in the English department, I had seen her and I knew that she was a lesbian. I knew a guy in the department and he asked me if I had ever read Sue's thesis and I said, 'No.' He said, 'It's just beautiful, but all the poems are to women.' At graduation, Sue asked me if I'd like to go over to a bar. We went and got pretty high. Then she said why didn't I go home with her. So I went with her and that was the beginning of that.

"About three weeks ago, my mother had this big gumbo. And we had a very nice party with people from the school. I said to my mother that since we had entertained all these people, I want to do something for my special friends. So my mother, who is eighty years old, said, 'I understand you have a different lifestyle.' It like to killed me. All these damn years I've wasted trying to keep it from her. We had the party and everybody thought it was just wonderful.

"My mother could not stand Sue at first. She thought it was all Sue's fault. Somebody else is taking me and I'm not like that. Sue hung in there and eventually they became friends. I think my oldest son understands this whole thing. My youngest son—I don't think it has ever dawned on him. Both of them have known Sue most of their lives, and I think both of them love her. My grandkids love her. My children grew up with my mother, and both sons are very successful and I'm very proud of them. I don't think this relationship has hurt them in any way.

"I am also out at work. I know everybody knows. We were the talk of the department for about a week. Then we just settled in. My department head knows about it and she appointed me to be her assistant. I guess it doesn't bother her.

"My advice for other women who are thinking about a change in their sexual orientation is to go for it. Now there are so many opportunities. Twenty-one years ago we were very isolated. We didn't know there were organizations—and there weren't many. Today, I see many avenues open to the young,

15

and they don't need to be in the closet. There are groups to help them come out if they are willing to take that chance."

Carole

*I felt that I was supposed to be married . . . All the while, I
really wanted to jump the fence and be with women.*

Carole is 37. She was born in Houston, Texas. She has a B.S. degree
in nursing and 21 hours of graduate school. She is working as a nurse.

"The first time I was married I was 27. I was dating this guy
and he was dying to get married. I had only known him for nine
months and one day I decided, 'O.K., let's get married.' And
we were married three weeks later.

"I'm a recovering alcoholic and there was a lot of drinking
in that marriage that didn't really help. Two months later, I
dumped spaghetti in his shoes, chased him around the apartment with a butcher knife, and then picked up and left.
Looking back on it, it's pretty funny, but it wasn't at the time.

"That was the first marriage. We fought a lot. We drank a
lot. Once I was married, I didn't want to have sex. I don't know
what else to say. It was just crazy behavior.

"My second marriage ended five years ago when I was 31.
It lasted nine months. I knew him for a month before I married
him. I was afraid if I didn't do it very fast I'd change my mind.

"I've been engaged five times and chickened out. This man
was an alcoholic, too. We drank our way through nine months.
I finally realized it was a pretty sick relationship and it ended
up with me being badly battered. It was the turning point in my
life. I decided that I couldn't drink like that anymore. I couldn't
deal with men anymore. So I joined AA and started my
recovery.

"I felt that I was supposed to be married. I thought I would
be accepted better if I were married. All the while, I really
wanted to jump the fence and be with women. But I was too
scared. All those years I was trying to force myself to be what
I thought I was supposed to be. I'm sorry I waited so long.

17

"The first woman I went out with was my bus driver—I made a pass at her. I used to catch this bus to work. Evidently, they rotate drivers every couple of months and I knew this would be her last run. I was so fascinated with this women I didn't know what to do, so I invited her to lunch and gave her my business card. So, she called me at work, and then took me to a casino one night. I wore the most un-lesbian-like outfit— a skirt and this real frilly little blouse—and she was embarrassed and she made me go home and change my clothes. I was so nervous. We're still friends now.

"Now, I'm in a long-term relationship—I feel married. Lucy and I got together nine months ago. I never thought I'd have a relationship with anybody like this. She is my soul mate. I don't know what else to say about it. It just works. I met her through mutual friends at a dinner party, and it was love at first sight! It was just one of those things—we saw each other across the room.

"At first I wasn't sure how I felt about the transition from a heterosexual orientation to lesbianism. I thought maybe it was curiosity—some sort of acting out. I had to be sure it was for the right reasons. I hated men and was afraid of them and I wasn't sure that I wanted things to be this way. I had had social pressures and I wanted to be accepted. Well, I went ahead with it.

"I stuck with the first woman because she was my entry into the community. Little did I know that lesbians were everywhere! I just didn't know. I started coming out to my straight friends, and the ones who knew me the longest said they figured this would happen. They thought the battering would be the thing that pushed me over.

"My best friend, who lives in Dallas, has a lot of those stereotypes, and she won't let me bring Lucy to her house for fear that Lucy will molest her children. She says that she is not going to tell her husband. We are still friends but he doesn't know that I'm gay. I think in the beginning she kept hoping that I would come to my senses.

"The same is true with my family. I came out to my brothers pretty early on. They were cool about it, but they felt that it was just a phase. I came out to my mother about two years ago. She suspected but didn't want to see it. Again, she thought it would be a phase. She is now seeing that this a permanent change. She liked Lucy until she figured out what was going on, and then, she did a 180 degree turn. I'm out to some people at work because they are gay, too. I'm out to my friends—where I live. The guy next door knows.

"I didn't have any children because I had had my tubes tied, and the only relationship I have with my former husbands is through my lawyer, who is my father. I wouldn't let my second husband know about me because I'm still afraid of him. The less I have to do with him the better. I sued him and won but I've haven't seen any money. My only concern about him is that he not batter other women. That is really scary to me. I was his third wife—I didn't know that. His battering seemed to get worse and worse and I'm concerned that he'll kill the next one.

"As far as the future, I plan to be with the same partner. I'd like to be in a job where I'm out. It's getting harder and harder. I suppose I could maintain this masquerade forever but, I don't like it. I'm a feminist, too. I went to my first feminist lecture recently. It was Sonia Johnson and I thought I was going to die! I'd like to be in some situation where I could be more outspoken like that.

"My advice for women contemplating a change in their sexual outlook is to just do it. I kick myself for waiting so long. A lot of misery could have been avoided. All of this feminist stuff has really opened me up. I'm just sorry I waited this long. I love being a lesbian."

Marlene

For me, it was a long mental, moral and religious struggle.

Marlene is 52. She was born in Louisiana. She was a bank officer and is now retired.

"I was married twice. The first time was in 1957. He was my high school sweetheart and he had been in the service, and I was very much in love with him. We had one child. We were married a couple of years, then divorced. After being laid off at work, he found a new job that took him away from my parents' home where we were staying. He just came home on weekends, and then he started fooling around with other women.

"My first relationship with a woman started shortly after I had just divorced my first husband in 1959, and I needed a roommate. From that roommate situation we finally became lovers. I felt very confused and very guilty. The first encounter that we had, I cried and cried my heart out. I felt we had committed an unpardonable sin. I was raised strict Southern Baptist and it went against everything I believed. I could not make any sense out of it. Nothing about it was logical to me. It was something that was just so foreign. I didn't know anybody else like that. I had never read about it. I could not comprehend it.

"We split up several times in the years to follow, but we were together a total of seventeen years. After about 10 years we decided that we should not do that—that we should turn our lives around. So we got married to men. That was when I married for the second time. Of course, this marriage was done for all the wrong reasons. I believe the guy was in love with me, but I was still in love with this woman. And so, a year later, we were divorced. For me, it was a long mental, moral and religious struggle.

"The first woman lover that I had for seventeen years passed away. Then I had a second lover for four years. But, I

20

was grieving and was on the rebound, and I should never have gotten into that relationship. After about a year, I realized that I was not really in love with this person. I told her that, and from then on, it was more of platonic relationship. "I have never discussed my lifestyle with my son. I feel in my heart that he does know. How could he not know? He's 32, and people today are more wise to things like that. I've always talked with him about whomever I've lived with as if they were a part of my life. Neither of my previous husbands know about me. I have a sister and a brother. We have never discussed it, but I strongly suspect that they know. I don't know whether my parents know or not. I think if anyone told them they would just deny it. I have no desire to tell them.

"I am out to my friends, but I really don't have any friends who are not gay. All the years that I worked I kept my lifestyle from others. Then after I retired, I didn't worry about that anymore. It was hard because I had some straight friends that I really cared about and I would have liked to have been able to share that with them. Since I stopped working, I have not retained those friendships.

"I sought counselling two years ago after I had broken up with a woman I had been with for nine years. I was in therapy for about 13 months trying to get over that relationship. I had some personal problems, too, because I've been in really bad health for five years. I have rheumatoid arthritis and I'm a diabetic. I had to take an early retirement because of my health, and I had to deal with the issue of not having a career any more. I really liked what I was doing—I was in banking.

"I think women contemplating a change in lifestyle should go to a counselor—someone who they can talk to, someone with good advice. People need to be aware of the hard side of gay life. Society is set up for straight people, and it is important to be aware that it's not going to be easy. But, knowing the facts, if a woman wants a change her lifestyle, that's what she should do.

"Young lesbians seem to have it more together and I think they have more opportunities than we older ones. In today's society, people seem to let you do what you want to do. What

I see in the younger lesbians is that they play the field so much and are so loose with their sexuality. I'm not sure that's a good thing. But, maybe I put too much emphasis on that. It's just that there is a lot more to a relationship than sex.

"I am in a relationship now that is over two years old and it's going well. I would like to have better health but I don't expect to, and we are doing well in spite of it."

Nancy

*I made a decision to become a lesbian based on the fact
that I was in the fifth generation of very strong women.*

Nancy is 43. She was born in White Plains, New York. She had two
years of college and owns two very successful businesses.

"I was married five years to the day: November of 1968 to
November of 1973.

"I married my high school sweetheart and I also put him
through college, where he got two degrees in architecture. His
name was Jerry and we were very kindred spirits—very entre-
preneurial. We were both natives of Dallas and both from very
wealthy families. We went to a city where we had no attach-
ments to see what we were made of, and both of us became
successes in our respective businesses.

"Then, on the day of our anniversary as Jerry and I were
talking, I learned that he wanted a divorce. I left that day and
we were divorced two days later. I was devastated. He had
given me no clues at all. I loved the marriage and I was very
relationship oriented. I never wanted children, and we didn't
have any. What I see during this last 17 years since I was
married is that Jerry wanted to see what he could do without
a strong woman. His mother was a very strong woman and I
am too. I think he wanted to see what he could do on his own.
Now our relationship is friendly—but very perfunctory. We
celebrated our high school reunion together, and I see him
periodically. He remarried six years ago and that marriage has
just ended.

"I consider myself very much a lesbian now. In 1978, I was
very promiscuous with men, but I would still fantasize about
women. I had a lot of close friends who were lesbians.

"In 1980, I made a decision to become a lesbian based on the
fact that I was in the fifth generation of very strong women, and
I was in a female business—I always worked very well with

23

women. Many people have challenged me on that decision, and I have had to deal with a lot of shame about being a lesbian. Once I made the decision, I became celibate. I traveled for two years around the world by myself to think about whether or not this was a good decision for me.

"I decided it was a good decision, and when I came back home, I asked my lesbian friend to introduce me to this lesbian woman. I had heard about her for years and I asked her to support me in getting into the lesbian community. I met this woman whom I had never met before, and we became lovers for the next eight years. I was enthralled with the mystique of it. There was the thrill of that which was taboo.

"Then reality set in. I thought something was wrong with me because I was gay. This was a very serious change that I had made. I abandoned all my straight friends. I felt that I was not in a position to go to them and tell them about my lifestyle change. The more I became committed in this relationship, the more I realized the shame.

"Three years into the relationship I went into therapy and programs for alcoholism and compulsive overeating. I was a very compulsive person and I would go on some binges now and again. There was a time there when I was drunk for three months, and then I realized I needed to go into AA. I had had a marijuana addiction in the late seventies that I stopped on my own. I had also been a prescription drug addict.

"When I made the decision to go into AA, I could finally look at all that. I had tremendous difficulty dealing with the shame of those early years. The therapy and groups helped greatly. As a result of my AA work, I went to my straight friends and told them how wrong I was to cut them out of my life. I told them I was gay, and, of course, they knew. I still had a lot of guilt about it. My relationship ended in May of 1988 when she left me for our best friend who was a women 20 years younger than I. I was devastated!

"To help me with the depression from the breakup, I went into a treatment center in Arizona for a 22-day program. Mostly, I needed an arena from which to tell my family. It was the first time I had been in a lot of pain and I felt I couldn't go to my sisters and my brother, and I felt very sad about my dishonesty. When I talked with them, the response was excellent. They were very supportive and very nurturing, and they have never discussed it since!

"My family makes constant homosexual jokes, and I guess it is unrealistic to have them accept my homosexuality. The fact that they have not accepted it is just not my problem. They didn't cut me off. If I got in trouble, I know I could turn to my family. I am the youngest of four children with stepbrothers and stepsisters. I am the least outgoing of the four. It's a strong group. I am my parents' favorite child. I was very relieved to get that secret out.

"Somewhere around three years ago I finally made peace with being gay. I am out to just about everyone who is important to me in my life. I do not broadcast it, but, if there is a need to tell someone in the course of a friendship, I tell. It is very easy.

"I had this eight-year relationship in which I was monogamous. When she left, I had relationships with four women in a three-month period of time. I have been with a total of seven women, but for about four years I have had no relationships. I am seeing that there is greater need for me to be alone and to learn to be alone. I am now some 60 pounds overweight, and that is just another indication that I'm not ready to be in a relationship. I'm covering up too much. That's my suit of armor. I'm pretty much at peace, but, on the whole, I love being in a relationship. I would hope that I'd soon be in another one. Finally, after three years, I'm letting go of that eight-year relationship that I had. I have found out how to nurture myself.

"My advice to women contemplating a change is look at the consequences of what you are doing. It is a major change. There is a tremendous responsibility that comes with that. There is being out, and there is outing others. I have far more respect for lesbians' confidentiality now than when I was straight.

"Secondly, just do what is right for you. I have been fortunate that I finally learned to accept my homosexuality. It took a lot of dollars and a lot of pain to accept myself. One other bit of advice is don't gossip about other lesbians. It is too close-knit a group. I have been both the offender and recipient, and there can be much damage.

"I have found that the only time I have ever been discriminated against in my life was by lesbians. I don't seem to look like a lesbian so I'm not always accepted as a part of the group. I don't fit the stereotypical view. The reality is that I just have a lot of fear. I have not made myself be a part of the group, and, consequently, I think they look at me with some fear. There is so much enmeshment within the lesbian community that I can go to a dinner party with eight lesbians and six of them will have been with other people at that party. It seems incestuous to me.

"I am not as goal-oriented as I used to be. That puts pressure on me that does not serve me well. I am, in some ways, living one day at a time. I don't project that much in the future; however, I do see myself being in a long-term relationship. That is my hope. I see being in my consulting business. I see having a lot of money. If I never worked another day in my life, I would be thrilled. I see a very simple world in the future. I have been so high profile and I was not that happy.

"Where I find my serenity and my contentment is in a small world with a close support group. I do hope it's with a partner and yet I'm content to not have a partner if that seems to be the right course for me."

Jocelyn

*I'm very blessed . . . and I feel very sad for that young girl
that I was.*

Jocelyn is 62. She was born in Galveston, Texas. She is a drug and
alcohol counselor and owns a retreat center.

"I was 19 when I first married in 1948. I was married for 25
years and had six children.

"It ended because he was a gambler; at least, I want to
blame it on that. We got married because it seemed to be the
thing to do. I was running away from home and my alcoholic
father. In hindsight, I think I was also running away from my
own sexual stuff.

"When I was in college I was seduced by a woman, and I
found it very confusing. I thought, 'Well, at least I won't get
pregnant.' Pregnancy was a big issue in those days. I was very
high Episcopalian, and, one time, when I went to confession
the priest told me I wouldn't get in any trouble no matter what
I told him and I lied. Thank goodness I had enough sense to do
that!

"I was in pre-med but couldn't afford medical school, so I
went into nursing school. Then John and I started dating. He
was very clever and a lot of fun. I was an only child and had
been lonely, and I remember always wanting lots of children,
and I could see that he liked kids. I wanted to show my parents
how families should be done. So I married John.

"We had only dated six weeks, but he was very assertive
and I wanted to have someone sweep me off my feet. I went to
work and he finished school. He got his degree in engineering
and I helped him get his company started. I was twenty-one
when I had my first child. Then I had six children in nine years.
We got to be a good little family—went to church and the
whole bit.

"John was a gambler, and it got progressively worse. I started seeing a therapist to straighten my husband out. And it turned out that the therapist was a sex addict. It was a man. He was inappropriately sexual with me and I went right along with it. Now I know it was because I had been sexually abused as a child. He had group and he encouraged the group to hug each other. Then we had parties and we would go swimming in the nude. And the group would always go out drinking.

"My own drinking was increasing at this time. I was a binge drinker. I would go to Las Vegas with my husband and I would drink. At a holiday party, I would just get awfully drunk and become very sexual and flirt with all the guys. One time we had a suite at one of the hotels downtown and I got very very drunk. The hotel suite had a grand piano in it, and I went knocking on doors trying to find someone to play the piano. I finally came to this place where these two couples were, and one of the guys said, 'Yes, I can play the piano.' He went on down to the room and his girl was there laying on the bed and I propositioned her. Thank God she didn't take me up on it! When I would be drunk these things would come out.

"My marriage was deteriorating. John's gambling was getting worse and I was in this group doing very inappropriate things. John's game had been that when he won big, I would get half of it for whatever I wanted. I would fix up the house or things that ordinarily would get done anyway. I was beginning to be a little more independent.

"So, one year when I was about 44, he won a lot of money. I got all the kids taken care of and I went off on an adventure to a dig in Africa. It was wonderful and it was the first time in my life I hadn't been someone's daughter, or mother, or wife, or teacher. It was a wonderful trip. There were 17 people and I learned that I could like myself and enjoy being by myself. It was a real marker in my life.

"Right after that, my marriage really deteriorated, and I got a divorce. Then I started having an affair with this man who was from the therapy group. He was about 20 years older than I. My alcoholism really got going good, and I did a lot of acting out. I was still with this group and we had group sex and everything. For me, it was just an excuse to be with another woman. I lived such a double life.

"Then, in 1979, I met Bob, who was a fine upstanding man. He represented decency, and he was so different from how my life was. Eventually, after five years, we got married. I finally broke away from the therapist. Bob was also an alcoholic. In marrying him I knew I could drink as much as I wanted to, yet, the girl in me thought she was going to cure her father. His drinking got worse. Bob had had a very tragic life. One of his sons killed himself while on drugs six months after his mother, Bob's wife, had died. This son was gay and had just found out he was HIV positive. Bob was homophobic.

"When Bob and I got married, we both got into recovery. About two years later, Bob got lung cancer. He died about six or seven years ago, and then, six months after Bob died, his other son killed himself. That whole thing was a Shakespearean tragedy. I had a lot to work through, but I stayed in recovery.

"The first time I ever felt sexual toward a woman was back when I was 10 or 12, which seemed normal at that time. Being a lesbian is complicated. Once in the recovery group with Bob I said that I was bisexual. I know lesbians don't think you can be bisexual, but I think you can!

"A few years ago, I opened a retreat center. A good friend of mine came out and lived with me. She was such a help in opening that retreat. We lived together for a long time, and we finally became sexual with each other. I was really thrilled and it was really good. She was a wonderful person and I am still friends with her. We have a lot of work to do, but we are thinking about getting back together some day.

"I was really ready to be pretty open about being a lesbian, but she wasn't sure she was lesbian. I found out later that she had had an affair with a younger woman in college. She was really depressed and confused at the time. She went into treatment and started working on her own problems. Then she came back and we were very miserable. About six months later she left and got a good job. The separation was very painful for both of us. She nearly killed herself, but she also got to work on her own stuff. She is now in a pretty damned good place. We see each other and we go out.

"In the last year I have told four of my kids about my sexuality. It was hard for me. I also think all the secrecy was hard on my relationship. I thought, 'Here I am in a 12-step program, and I'm a counselor.' I finally went to Cottonwood for a month to work on my sexual abuse. The whole thing is that you are as sick as your secret. After that I thought I needed to tell my kids.

"The oldest one had a friend who was lesbian. I told her that I might have a relationship with a woman. She said that she suspected that, and she was easy about it. Next, I told another daughter, and she is praying for me. She thinks it's evil and not natural and so forth. However, it hasn't ruined our relationship.

"Then I told my oldest son. His wife had known for a while. I told him that I was working on my sexuality now and that I thought I was gay. He said 'Mom, I want to tell you that there was a time when I wondered about myself.' He told me that it was O.K. and that he understood. He was more worried about his career and family that what I was doing sexually. He said it was nobody's business.

"Then I told my hippie son and his wife together. He said, 'I wondered what you were doing for sex.' Then his wife said that she'd had an affair with a woman once. They were wonderful.

"I still have two children I haven't told. One is far away and the other is a fundamentalist Christian, and I'm not sure I'd have such a nice reception there.

"I know I'm more attracted to women than men. In some ways it makes it easier to deal with men because I'm not looking at them as sex objects or take-care objects.

"I'm not out and I'm not closeted. If it is appropriate, I tell people, and with others it is none of their business. I don't think God is going to get me. I think, too, at my age—how many men are left? It's almost a practical thing if you are sexual. I have read books which discuss older women deciding to be sexual with women. Women are more open. Most of the men I know in this part of the world are pretty rednecked.

"I'm 62 and just now am beginning to give myself permission to have fun. I have my bachelor's in education and then I've taken the hours required for drug and alcohol counseling. I've studied with various people in counseling.

"My work at the present time is that I have a retreat facility. People come out and do workshops or do weddings. I also come into town three days a week and counsel with women, particularly women who have been sexually abused. I love my work in counseling. I want to give myself more permission to write and paint. I would like to find a partner—a fairly healthy person to live and enjoy life with.

"My advice for women who are contemplating a change of lifestyle is to get into support groups. Talk to people. Read books. Build up your self-esteem. Learn to accept yourself.

"If the relationship has to be a secret, then I think there is a mark against it. I think you should not be closeted. When I told some close friends, they were hurt that I hadn't told them.

"I have come out a lot in the past year and everyone has been very nice. Of course I am still very selective about who I tell! I'm very blessed and I feel very sad for that young girl that I was. I'm also very glad I had my kids."

Gail

Once I became involved with a woman, I realized that was what I wanted for the rest of my life.

Gail is 42. She was born in Bridgeport, Connecticut. She has a B.A. in Russian.

"When I first realized I was gay I didn't do a whole lot about it. I was both guilty and confused.

"It happened at a time in life where my job allowed me to just sit and think. After a while it occurred to me that I was no less a person of integrity. I was no less nice. I was polite. I was no less of a friend than I had been before. It was not very hard to accept it.

"That process took a few months; then it was done. I was in a marriage and I was not financially in a position to leave. There was no strong reason to leave. I was being treated so well.

"I was married 19 years because it was the thing to do. It was the only thing to do—I did not feel like there was any other alternative. I felt that I was in love for a while. My husband was going to graduate school and felt so guilty about me supporting him that he took over all the household tasks. That never changed once he got his Ph.D. I was not ever a housekeeper. We were very tolerant of each other and just kind of co-existed. It was boring. We did very little together. The only thing that made the marriage work was that he never forced me to stay home and I never tried to force him to go out and be sociable with me. We did that for a long, long time.

"But, once I became involved with a woman, I realized that that was what I wanted for the rest of my life. Then I was impatient to get out of the marriage. With this marriage, I probably could have stayed married and led two lives; but, I didn't want to live my life that way either. So I finally left and filed for divorce. I was involved with a women for a year and a half while I was still married and then she left me for another woman and after that I stayed married for another year. It took a while to make the transition and find a community.

"My ex-husband and I have never discussed this, but I'm sure he knows. When I was having my first affair with a woman, he was very tolerant. He never asked where I had been when I came in at 2:30 in the morning having been to the bar and smelling like smoke. He didn't want to know.

"My parents are still living and are in their seventies. I came out to my mom and she took it very hard. When I got divorced she thought I would find another man and give her a grandchild. She took it very hard, but she is adjusting. She wants what is best for me. When I told her this would make me happy—she wasn't real pleased but she said O.K. Then Mom said, 'Don't tell your father, it would kill him. Don't tell your brothers because they might let it slip to your father and it would kill him.' But, my dad has been guessing for a while. I was telling him about my new job and that it was a woman-owned company and he said, 'Is she a member of your crowd?' He knew without a doubt. They are not the type of parents who would disown me—never.

"I'm out in the community. I had a party a few weeks ago and got to invite 55 people. I'm not out in my work because I'm in a new job. In my previous job it was not an issue. Some people knew and some people didn't and I really didn't care who knew. I didn't expect any problems. There were other gay people there, and it was a very comfortable environment. I've been on TV—I've been on the news. I went marching in Austin and my face showed up on the Houston news. I belong to Heartsong, a lesbian chorus.

"I am not currently in a relationship, and I have mixed feelings about that. Sometimes I think it is wonderful because I have all my time to myself. Then, there are sometimes I just get so lonely—I wish I had somebody in my bed. There is a real duality about that. I attend lesbian groups to meet friends. Relationships for me either happen or they don't; I don't seek them out. Recently, there was one that just almost happened, then didn't. I don't worry a whole lot about whether I'm involved with somebody.

"Ten years from now I want to be running a retirement home for women. I'm not in a position to act on it yet. I think it is needed in the community, but it is a big project. I feel that to do this I'm going to have to go get a master's degree in healthcare administration. I want to know how to do it, and I want to do it well because I know people in the community will be investing in my project.

"My advice to young lesbians is to take care of your career. If you have financial freedom, you can buy other kinds of freedom. For women who are contemplating leaving their husbands—I have the same advice. Have your career in order first. I thought mine was; but it wasn't, so I have been suffering financially, although, I did do some things right. I had checking accounts and credit cards all in my own name for years. I'm proud of myself."

Rosalie

? delete

It seemed like a natural progression . . . although it was like diving off a high board.

Rosalie is 59. She was born in New York City. She graduated from a three-year nursing program and one-and-one-half years of anesthesia training. She is working as a nurse anesthetist.

"I have been married six times. Five husbands—six marriages. I was married twice to one man. I have been heterosexual my whole life. I never thought of anything else. I was very open and sensual and enjoyed my relationships with men as long as I was in courtship. I discovered that I was very good at courtship and not very good at marriage . . . not very good at prolonged intimacy.

"As far as I am concerned, there have been only two men in my life in the last 25 years. I almost don't consider the previous marriages. I was between 20 and 30 and they were very short lived. Nice girls got married. Nice girls didn't divorce. The next-to-last man was very nice. He taught me about the world. I was kind of in-tow as his mate at that point. We were married 12 years and had three children.

"When my son started first grade, I went back to school and took a refresher course and resumed my career. Going back to work put an enormous strain on the marriage, and we decided to get some counseling. In therapy it came out that we didn't have a good marriage, but he liked things the way they were and wanted to continue with it. It was my decision that we could not go on with this marriage.

"After that marriage, I married somebody who was extremely handsome and a hellava lot of fun. I found out that he was an ex-convict and an extremely dangerous man. He was a sociopath. It lasted for almost five years. Then it took a few more years for him to get out of my life. Even now he will call me now and then.

35

"I put on a hundred pounds during that time. He had said, 'If you ever gain weight I will divorce you.' I gained weight and he still wouldn't leave me. It has proved to be almost impossible to take the weight off. This relates to me with a woman as well. It is a barrier between me and intimacy. I like living alone. . . . I mean I really like living alone. I am financially independent. I like having close friends, but it is very scary to let anybody get too close.

"I'm not sure whether I am a lesbian now or not. I have loved and had a relationship with one woman. That was about three years ago. We met at a feminist group and we began as friends. She was married at the time and it never occurred to me that she was a lesbian. The better we got to know each other, the closer we got. We became such good friends and so close—such mingling of minds and holding hands and breathing together. It seemed like a natural progression . . . although it was like diving off a high board. It was very scary. I even scared the hell out of her one day by calling her up at the office and telling her that I wanted to make love to her.

"We had a very powerful, passionate relationship. But, it was very scary, and I just had to back off from that intense closeness, and we somehow managed to salvage our friendship. We are now very good friends and are a support system for each other. We were together less than a year.

"I don't have any intimate relationships now. I have a couple of very good friends, and they are women. I don't like most men because I cannot stand to be patronized. I have discovered that when I'm with a man, I become so cute. I get into that old sixties garbage and I hate it. I don't mean it. It is all a part of my liking to conform. I don't think there is a chance in hell of my conforming anymore because I like being with women. I'm involved with lesbian women. As the old saying goes, 'If it quacks like a duck and looks like a duck, it must be a duck!'

"I have not had any more lesbians relationships, but I have discovered a very interesting thing. I'm a hundred pounds overweight. At one time in my life if I walked into a room, men noticed and wanted to be with me. That no longer happens

36

unless I'm sitting having a conversation, and they discover I am interesting to be with. They have to get past a very overweight woman. This isn't the case with women. I seem to attract younger women. It is fun.

"I don't consider myself out. I'm very closeted. To my children, my work, and so on. I have three children, from 25 to 30 years of age. Two of them are married and one is a lesbian. The only person I am out to is my lesbian daughter who knows exactly what I'm doing. Otherwise, it's nobody's business.

"I've been at work for 19 years, and everybody has known me through the last two marriages and as mother and grandmother. They think I'm asexual. They know I have women friends and that is all they expect of me. I have two best friends and we go to bars on occasion.

"Mostly, I'm very much of a hermit. I'm very happy this way. I don't know if it'll be the same after I retire. I might want to be with people more. Yeah, I lead a double life, and I'm not conflicted. I was always a little left of center anyhow, so what the hell. I am so fulfilled in what there is in my life that I don't feel the need to change. I'm very open to what ever happens and what ever brings me pleasure. A little less convention doesn't blow me away.

"If more women had their finances in their own hands things might be different. If you have money, you have power."

Anna

There was no word for lesbian at the time, and no one told me I was doing anything strange.

Anna is 40. She was born in Oklahoma City. She has had three years of work-related college classes. She works in a landfill gas field, monitoring the gas that is generated by the garbage.

"I was married September 10, 1969. My marriage was really boring. I think I was married to the idea of being married. I think it lasted as long as it did because my ex was in the military, and he was gone a lot. We started having a lot of problems when he got out of the Marine Corps and we had more time together.

"We had two children. I was four months pregnant when we married. My oldest son is now 22 and the youngest is 20. My marriage was boring, but at the time, I didn't know it was boring; I thought everybody was like that.

"I didn't know what an orgasm was. I was married three and a half years before I actually had one.

"I think the most satisfying thing about the marriage was the time I spent alone. Even when my kids were there, it was still a quiet kind of time. I had access to all the reading material I could possibly want. My husband thought I was reading too much of that awful feminist literature and blamed it for the decline of the marriage.

"During the first five years of my marriage, 80 percent of my time was spent alone. When I look back on my marriage, I find that time kind of strange. I was legally married for 11 years, but we separated for the last three.

"I do consider myself a lesbian now. I have ever since my first adult physical and emotional encounter with a woman. I had encounters when I was a child ... hugging and kissing with a girl friend who lived next door to me. I thought this was the most common, normal thing to do. My brother was there and it didn't seem to bother him. It just went on and I had experiences after that, too. In fact, everywhere I lived there seemed to be some female child in the neighborhood that I was cuddling with. That went on until junior high school. There was no word for 'lesbian' at the time and no one told me I was doing anything strange.

"My first relationship with a woman came when I was 27. I was separated from my husband, but we hadn't divorced yet. I was living with a woman and a man who worked at the same place I did. They had been living together for about eight years and were just about to get married. We had rented a large house together. I'm black, and they had a group of racially mixed friends that I became involved with.

"Anyway, there was this woman who I noticed that people in our group seemed to keep a little bit of a distance from. I didn't think much about it one way or the other. She just seemed to be this man's lover and he had several different lovers at different times. But anyway, I noticed a connection between this woman, Laurie, and me; but I didn't know just what it was.

"Then, later, a kind of weird thing happened. I was bowling on a league, and there were four of us women who were going to go out after bowling that night. I had had an accident that day when playing softball and had a head injury. When we started to go pick up this other woman, I got sick. I felt nauseous and had a throbbing headache, so I told them to go ahead and I would just stay there and sleep. I happened to be at this couple's house. Anyway, I stayed there, and they went out.

"When I woke up at about 3 a.m., there was Laurie—in bed with me. We started to talk, and the next thing I knew we were making love. I knew that her boyfriend, George, was in the living room but I didn't really care at that point. That's how it started.

"It was extremely intense for me. I didn't realize what was happening at that time. I became a real pest where she was concerned; I would just not let go. I was later told that she had

had encounters with other women in that group of friends. She just enjoyed having those encounters.

"I really liked it, and just didn't want to let go. I tracked her down to wherever she moved; I sent flowers and balloons to her at her job. She didn't return my phone calls or anything. It took me about six months to come to my senses and start to get over that. I had just about done it when I got a phone call from her at work and it started all over again. Anyway, she finally married and moved to California, and that was the last I saw of her. I actually went to the reception.

"That was the beginning for me because I found no interest in men after that. I was seeing one man in particular once before that. I wasn't in love with him but I enjoyed the time we spent together and I enjoyed sex with him. I enjoyed how sensitive he was. We could talk and I'd never had that with a man before. I had a couple of one-nights with guys that were just awful. That was all before Laurie.

"After Laurie, I was running from therapist to therapist trying to figure what the hell was going on. I didn't really have a name for it. I guess at the time I didn't think I was a lesbian. Of the first three counselors I saw, I seemed to be talking about only half of myself. That was the part that had been married and the childhood part. There was a whole other part that dealt with the experiences with girls when I was young. I didn't deal with the complete me.

"One friend finally suggested that I call the Lesbian Hot-Line to find a counselor to deal with that. At that time I was still kind of in the throes of Laurie. I wanted to find a way of being over that, so I called the Hot-Line and they gave me the name of three therapists. I settled on one and I saw her for about five years. It was through her that I got involved with the lesbian community. I finally knew that I was a lesbian and had to deal with that.

"It was very difficult to deal with those feelings because there is just no place to take them. Although I was separated at the time, people still thought of me as heterosexual and married. That closed down support from friends and people that I knew.

"After about six months of counseling, my counselor suggested an encounter group. I joined that and made friends. One of the women in that group took me to a gay bar. I didn't know that gay bars existed. After that, my social life seemed to revolve around the women that I met. I went to parties that were given by lesbians. I went out to the bars with other lesbians. Now my relationships are with other lesbian women.

"I am not currently in a relationship. I am emotionally involved with someone, but we are not in a relationship. This is very difficult for me—because this is a woman who is married. Her husband took a job in another state, and she moved with him. If she had stayed here, I doubt if the relationship would have ended; I think it would have continued in some kind of way. It's continuing now. We still have phone conversations, and I'm still trying to get her to see me some time. I can't deal with the idea of ending it completely. I can't not have a connection with this woman.

"I should say that this is one of the most difficult positions I have ever been in. I find I call her every two weeks. I can't bring myself to say that I don't want any contact with her. Now, I'm trying to get her to meet me in Arizona later this month.

"I don't consider myself really out because I'm not out at work. I think my ex-husband knows. I came out to my dad a few months ago. I have no sisters and have little contact with my brother. My children have known since I knew. I had to tell them because I wanted an open relationship with them. My oldest son was 12 at the time. My sons adjusted to the change really well. I had two lovers that my sons were involved with. We even took trips together. With other people, it's not very difficult to maintain secrecy; I'm pretty closed anyway.

"I can't look any further ahead than five years. I know that I want to be more settled in this part of the country. I want to be in a senior position with my job. I'd like to be working on my degree. And, I want to have my own home.

"I think one of the most important things that a woman thinking about a change can have is a support system. And, as a black woman who went through this, I think it's just extremely hard to have. There weren't a lot of black women there for me in the lesbian community. I need a space to deal with myself as a whole person—as a black lesbian mother."

Gayla

*I love men, and just, also, happen to love women. I found
my soul-mate in a woman.*

Gayla is 46. She was born in Pennsylvania. She has a B.S. degree in
music education, a M.A. in religious studies, and a Ph.D. in ministry.

"I was married in June of 1967, six days after I graduated
from college. I did all the right things. I got the degree and got
married and went to work. My first son was born three years
later and my second son was born two years after that. We also
took in a foster daughter when my eldest was eight. We had her
living with us until she finished high school and we had to
move away.

"I married, yet I was aware of having difficulties with men.
I had been raped four different ways by four different men
before I was married. I had told my husband when we were
courting that I was aware that I might not be able to be in a
relationship with a man after those experiences. He felt that it
was going to be O.K. He had a lot of faith in me and in what we
were doing. I had a lot of respect for him, and so we got
married. While I had feelings of warmth and respect for him,
I don't know whether I was in love or not. It is really hard to say.

"I had had this wild Latin fellow interested in me at the
same time, and he thought he was going to get me over all my
hang-ups—but I wasn't sure I wanted to get over all my hang-
ups. In contrast to him, Bob was kind, steady, and had a pretty
clear picture of what he wanted to do in life. His values
coincided with mine.

"Bob had come from a very strange family situation and
wanted family and loved my family. He was very much
attracted to the way my family operated. I think he married my
family as much as me. It was the image.... We were a big, noisy,
very tightly-connected family. It was nice, and it still is. I
admire and respect a lot of my brothers and sisters. I had a great

deal of respect for my father and, while I had a difficult relationship with my mother, I also respected her intelligence.

"The marriage, however, was one of those difficult situations. He is from a Scandinavian background, and his stepfather had abused him. So he had some difficulties with relationships. If I got too affectionate, he would do something silly to distance himself. I'm a very physical person and I like contact and touch. He was very patient and undemanding and gentle and very sexy. The combination was very attractive and the relationship was very satisfying sexually. We seemed to have an equal sexual drive. He had a wonderful body and still does. In our relationship, our physical relationship just got better and better but our emotional relationship did not. He was very private man and he preferred to do things alone.

"After two years we moved to Detroit and I was pregnant. We raised our sons and took on a foster daughter. That was very challenging because she was sexually ambivalent. She really pushed all my buttons and challenged all my issues. She was extremely intuitive so she read a lot in me that was accurate and hard to come to terms with. I had been very relieved that my second child was a son. I didn't want to bring a girl into the world. I didn't think the world was very responsive to females. We had the girl for three years when I decided to go into the ministry; my husband changed jobs, and we moved out of state.

"With this move, he reconnected with his father and sisters and he got a little warmer emotionally. Then it wasn't too much later that he asked me for a divorce. I knew he was involved with another woman. He said, 'Maybe I can stop hurting you.' So, at some level he was aware of some of my pain. I don't think he had the capacity to be emotionally supportive, given his own emotional background. That was an arid part of my life, and I sought intense female companionship because of it.

"Relatively early in our marriage, I became aware that he was looking around at other women, but he had always said that he was committed to family and he behaved that way for a time. Then it became really obvious that he was looking; that's when things started to go. It was my first ministry and he was not accustomed to my being the center of attention. We went through mediation divorce. We didn't want the children pulled every which way by the break-up. He wanted to be fair financially, and I think he was in so far as he was able. As much as I was in pain, I had an awareness that fighting in the courts wasn't going to change the pain. It was hard! Both of us were very clear about our obligations to our children. He still is; he is helping support them through college. He maintains close contact with those boys. We were married just short of 20 years.

"Even before I got married, I was conscious that I found both men and women physically attractive. I have a sense now that both my parents were bisexual, and they had gay and lesbian people come to our house. We knew it; it wasn't a secret. I grew up on the East Coast, New York metropolitan area, where there were openly gay people.

"When I was about seven I was a tomboy. So I was always with the guys and many times it was older guys. Because of that I was sexually active at a very young age, and I came as close to intercourse as you can get with immature males. I enjoyed it immensely. I thought it was wonderful. I liked the physical contact. So I was aware of being sexually compatible with men from seven or eight. It was in pre-puberty I was aware that I was attracted to women also.

"In high school I had very intimate friendships with girls. I don't recall making love but I was obviously in love. I was in love with one of my counselors at Girl Scout camp. There was a woman who was a year older than I was in school. I was so impressed with her. I thought she was spectacular!

"In college, my freshman year, there was a senior who was also a French horn major who mentored me in some wonderful ways. She enjoyed my mind and there was no question that I was in love with her. I'm not sure where she was with that. We used to kid around about it because we were both aware of the implications of the time we spent together. We were not intimate. I fell in love with all kinds of women. It was all sort of progressive. It's hard to say where it starts.

"I also fell in love with several men and women during my marriage. I, however, had a very strong code of honor about

45

behavior in marriage and I was not prepared to have an affair. But, I was aware I had feelings, even though I did not act on them.

"There were two major lesbian relationships in my life prior to the one I have now. One was a much younger woman who seemed to bring out my nurturing instincts. It was very confusing, and we were not sexual. Then there was a woman more than 10 years older than I with whom I was intimate. That was at a time when I realized that my husband was really looking elsewhere and I was trying to determine who I was and where I was. It was an experiment as much as anything. We had some real common spiritual beliefs, which was a very strong drawing point for me. So there were these two women who came at a very confusing time in my life. I felt neither would last, and, therefore, didn't give my full commitment; however, they were steps along the way for me.

"I met my present partner, Karen, when I was seeking my first settlement as a minister. Her husband was on the search committee. The committee called me to the church for an interview and she was working in the church as the administrator. The first time I looked into her eyes I thought, 'This is a person who is going to be very important in my life.' It has nothing to do with gender. It has to do with the individual and his or her spirituality. When Karen and her husband drove my husband and me back to the airport at the end of that week, I was aware of those vibrations and was very concerned about what I was getting into. We went back to Ohio for a month and then moved to Washington.

"Karen and I worked together as colleagues. One of the first things she did when I got into this ministry was to make it very clear that if it didn't work out for us to work in adjacent offices, she could be gone. She knew the congregation and was very supportive and helpful. As time went on, I was still having feelings for her, but I was also aware that we were both married. At this point, I put myself into therapy. I began to deal with family issues—and my sexuality.

"Karen was supervised by the board, not by me. We were sort of co-equals in the office. The set-up was very unusual. She told me that she hoped I felt safe and comfortable with her. Something in me snapped because I realized during therapy that feeling safe and comfortable was not something I had experienced in my life very often. While my household was in many ways very loving, it did not feel safe for me as the eldest and the responsible one. I was always in a performance mode. Eventually, I told Karen that I had feelings for her. She had been talking to a friend about how well we got along and he said to her, 'Look, if this were a man, you would know this was courting behavior.' He tried to get her to be more aware. She did not respond to my statement, except to say that she didn't know what she was going to do. That remained unchanged for years as I continued counseling and she was doing her own work. I finally asked her if she would be interested in persuing some spiritual work together. So we worked together as spiritual peers for several years, doing co-counseling work.

"My counselor said that I was doing all my work with Karen, and I just debriefed with her. That was true—because I felt I needed a neutral third party that I trusted to monitor my process. The potential for self-delusion in love relationships is so powerful. So we worked very hard as spiritual co-counselors, even going to retreats together.

"Somewhere in this process, my ex-husband found another woman. Actually she may be the perfect person for him, as she is as disinterested in public life as he is. The problem was that she was the mother of my son's girlfriend, and also in the church, and when they got together it caused a scandal in the congregation. Actually, my son stayed with his girlfriend until his father and her mother married. Then she couldn't deal with it, dating her 'brother.' They have both since married other people. My younger son calls the whole thing a soap opera. It was just awful. It's a miracle that I managed to stay in the ministry. I was so devastated by the way it went. It was terrible for me and the congregation. Karen was a rock through the whole thing.

"Anyway, during our spiritual mentoring she mentioned that I had been wandering around in her meditations five years before I showed up in the flesh. That's why our first meeting was powerful for both of us. Since she processes privately she didn't say anything about it for a long, long time.

"Sometime before my divorce, she told me that her marriage had been over for 10 years. Her husband had been engaged in a three-year affair and wanted a divorce. So, one month after their youngest graduated from high school, they filed for divorce. It was a very civilized, quiet divorce; they just did it. We had been through all this garbage. She saw me through my divorce and I saw her through hers. Suddenly we were able to be together and we just got closer and closer. We are now living together after some seven years of knowing each other. She moved near me and we finally bought a house together and finally we had our commitment service.

"Right now my professional life is falling apart and the relationship is keeping me together. It's very supportive. It's interesting because we both have very busy lives. She works in Seattle and commutes. She has a 12-hour day. I work in the town where we live. I'm a public person—very active in the community. I have meetings almost every evening. We make time to be together.

"I think the most heavenly time of the day is when we can just spend a few hours in the day snuggling up to each other in the evening. That time is just really special.

"Here in Seattle, I'm totally out. In the community where we live, I'm out only to the congregation. They were invited to our service. I'm in the process of a negotiated termination from my ministry, not just because of my lesbian lifestyle—although that is a part—but because of the intensity of my personal style . . . my East Coast style, in some ways. I think the congregation was just asked to go through too many changes with me. It is a very conservative group, and I think they reflect the community as a whole. The majority of them want me to stay, but it has become an untenable situation.

"I am out to my children. I was out long before I was in a relationship with Karen. My elder son is delightful about it. He had had a dear friend from childhood, who goes to his school, tell him that he was bi-sexual. He tried so hard to empathize with his friend. It was very touching when he came to me with his struggles with it.

"I told my husband in the process of the divorce, before I was in a relationship. He wasn't surprised. He tried very hard to tell me that it didn't change the way he felt about me. His feelings about me had more to do with my intensity and his difficulty dealing with that. He wanted someone who was more easy with life. He and his wife attended our service. All our kids were there for the service.

"I want to be very clear that I have very positive feelings about men. I have had male mentors professionally who were wonderful to me. I feel very warm toward my sons. That's one of my reasons for coming out to them. I feel that our society forces men into boxes that are just as constricting as women's boxes.

"Both sons are very sensitive to these issues. My younger son just wrote a paper on how difficult it is for a person of conscience to be a white male. I have a friendship with my sons as well as a parent relationship, and they are just precious to me. I see them facing a very hard time in the world. I love men and just also happen to love women. I found my soulmate in a woman.

"Five years from now, I see myself being with Karen. She is a life companion. I suspect that I'll have at least one more ministry, but I'm also hoping to be a published writer. I have four books of poetry that I'd like to send in. I would eventually like to be lecturing and traveling. It would be a ministry—but different than I have now."

Beth

Delete per request

It was like discovering that water was good to drink ... it was so easy, and so natural.

Beth is 51. She has a Ph.D. in biophysics, and a M.A. in pastoral counseling. She is in private practice in counseling and healing.

"I was married 14 years in my first marriage and divorced—no children. My next relationship was with Bob; we were together for 13 years. We never married. We have one child.

"Bob's an engineer and I was a scientist and we had a lot of intellectual abilities in common. We had good times, and we enjoyed each other. We were not seeing other people.

"After about six months, I got pregnant. I didn't think I could get pregnant at age 38, but I had always wanted a child. I decided I did not want to abort the child and said to Bob, 'This is the situation I am in.' Bob decided he would stay with me, but he wouldn't marry me. So we started out on that foot.

"I felt trapped ... that I had no other options with the child. I did not enjoy living with Bob at the beginning. It was really tough with this brand new child. The pregnancy was easy ... an easy birth. All of that was wonderful, but living with Bob was really difficult.

"I was very unhappy for a while. But then we kind of both changed a bit so we had some years that were very pleasant and focused on raising Jenny. In her little years it was just great.

"Then I changed careers—all of this happened very early in Jenny's life. Just on the other side of forty-five—after a near-death experience, I changed from a research scientist in a research lab to pastoral counseling, healing and spirituality.

"I didn't really talk to Bob very much about it. Then all of a sudden I changed from a really hard-core scientist, with no spiritual interest at all, to this 'woo-woo' spiritual stuff ... and

50

Bob found it hard to deal with. Our relationship continued, but with not much sharing about what was important.

"We played well together. We each ran our separate lives and business lives and came together around our daughter and vacations. It continued that way for years . . . until I met Judy.

"I first met Judy about three years ago while I was in graduate school for pastoral counseling. We gradually got to know each other, and the sense of closeness and emotional connection with her made the relationship with Bob seem like an absolute waste of time. He and I had grown quite apart, especially when I was in school.

"I was really busy working half-time and going to school the other daytime hours. In the evenings, I was studying and spending time with Jenny. I was realizing how separate my interests really were from Bob's. We had already put a tremendous amount of distance between us. We were just not on the same wavelength.

"Suddenly I felt this depth of connection with Judy that also became sexual and very much a surprise. It was as natural as anything. I had no idea that this depth of connection could be possible. It was like discovering that water was good to drink. It was so easy and so natural. I thought, 'This is a life partner that I have been looking for—for thousands of years.'

"We are having a hard time right now, Judy and I. With the stress of separating from Bob and trying to build a stable life for Jenny, my relationship with Judy has suffered. We have not been intimate for four months and I don't anticipate that we will—because she wants to be living together and really operating as a couple. I don't feel I can do that now because I'm trying to first create a stable life for myself and my daughter.

"This relationship with Judy has changed my life—it was so intense and so full. I am in limbo now as far as the relationship goes; I just have no idea where I'm going with it. We still see each other a lot.

"I waited a very long time to talk to any of my friends about this because I was still living with Bob. I don't think I talked to anybody because of that, except my counselor.

"I would like a relationship with someone who touches me as deeply as Judy has. I don't know whether that would be a man or a woman—and that doesn't make any difference to me. If it is Judy—if things open up and that relationship goes again—that would be fine. If it is another woman—that's fine. If it is a man, that's fine, too. But the quality of the relationship, the level of intimacy and ease is something I want. I don't know if I'll ever find that again. I can't settle for anything less than that depth.

"I have been honest with Bob; I told him I was leaving him and that I was having a relationship with a woman. He is still pretty angry at me. He said in counseling—we did some couples counseling—that it was easier for him that I had become involved with a woman than if I had been with another man. I thought that that said something about the level of importance he gives women.

"The sense of my own identity is coming out, so to speak. Then to have my daughter at this very delicate age of sexuality for her—it was just overwhelming. That may have a very big part in having to do with what I feel now—just backing up. I found in doing that that I have an awful lot of healing to do from the 13-year relationship with Bob.

"It's not just understanding it—I've come to that—but it's giving myself time to adjust. Jenny is doing so much acting out just now that she keeps me very busy responding to crises. A good part of it is teenage stuff and some of it is driven by some sense of betrayal and anger toward Bob and me.

"I am at that place where all the activity of change has happened and everything inside falls apart for awhile—and it hasn't all come back together again.

"It will be interesting to see whether I become part of a couple. I am enjoying being by myself, at least for awhile. Friends are important right now. We'll see what happens."

Annee

When I married my second husband, I already knew I had a real interest in women. But I thought it was all fantasy stuff and it would go away.

Annee is almost 40. She was born in Texas. She attended a community college and then graduated from a beauty college. She went on to more college classes, has a drafting certificate, and takes computer classes for design work. She works as a mechanical tool designer in electronics.

"In 1969, I married a man from Colombia, South America. I knew him only three months when I went with him to live there. The marriage was an escape from my parents' house. I was living in Louisiana, and we eloped and drove into Texas and got married. Then we took off and went to South America.

"I was very unhappy and emotionally sick there. There was the language barrier and I was very isolated. I had a lot of expectations about what marriage was supposed to be, and there were a lot of disappointments. He didn't want children and I did. We lived with his family, who were very vocal, and very passionate. In my home, we had to be very quiet around my father, so I wasn't used to all this hubbub. I got depressed and didn't do very well. I felt like a possession of his, and I didn't appreciate that. I felt that my only purpose was to provide a sexual outlet for him.

"I finally started attending a women's organization and I found out there was an underground system for American women who lived in Colombia. If you had children there, you couldn't leave the country without your husband's permission. I didn't have any kids, so that wasn't an issue, but my husband didn't want me to leave. After about two and a half years, I told him I wanted to go home and visit my parents and if he wouldn't let me, I'd go underground. He bought me a round-trip ticket. I got back here and got a job. I sent him money for a few months and sent back the other half of the ticket.

"There were really no repercussions from that. He called a lot, and finally threatened that he would get involved with drugs and be an addict. In the meantime, I got involved with drugs. I got a divorce about 10 years later. I was just too occupied with doing whatever I wanted to do. Eventually he did give me a divorce without any contest.

"The second time I married was in 1982. When I married my second husband, I already knew that I had a real interest in women, but I thought maybe it was just fantasy stuff and it would go away.

"I met him the night I decided to go and find where women were. I was feeling thwarted because I couldn't find the women's bar that I was looking for. I couldn't find the address and I was walking up and down the street and finally decided to go home. He sat down beside me on the bus, and we just started talking. Then we started spending more time together. It was a whirlwind relationship, and we just decided to get married.

"He was eight years younger. I felt that he was easily controlled and manipulated. There was a power imbalance, and I had more power. It wasn't good ultimately, but it was the first relationship where I had some power. I thought that he would be a ticket for me to have children. I had had a hysterectomy, but I still wanted to have kids.

"Before we got married, we talked about adoption. Within a month after we got married, he said to me, 'Let's go to the doctor and get you fixed so you can have kids.' I got out a medical book and sat down with him and explained to him why I couldn't have kids. When he realized I could not have children, it became a real issue. He wanted kids of his own. I still wanted kids, but he wouldn't adopt. About this time, I started having affairs with women. We weren't married three months when I started going to the Lesbian Resource Center for their weekly rap groups.

"I had done some experimentation with girls in high school. I had a real crush on one girl who the other students called a 'lesbian,' as if it were a dirty word. It sounded pretty

54

interesting to me, and just served to intensify my crush. Then, in the early '70s, I started having affairs with women. There was a man/woman couple that I knew and they asked if I wanted to have a menage with them and I thought, 'This is unique. Sure, I'll try this.' But, I soon realized I didn't want to have anything to do with him—I was having a great time with her. She and I were sexual a couple more times, but it was awkward because her husband didn't want to be left out.

"Then, shortly after my second husband and I were married, I really fell in love with a woman. And I finally knew that my real feelings belonged with women. It was wonderful! That relationship lasted for a year. It turned out that she was a heterosexual who was experimenting with me, all the while I'm telling her I love her. It was really heartbreaking for me. Of course, here I was married!

"My husband worked weekend nights, so it was relatively easy for me to be out and about the women's community. And I would fabricate car breakdowns and other excuses to be away as much as possible. It ended because she got tired of waiting for me to end my marriage, and when I finally did, she was ready to move on. While she was not the love of my life, she was a stepping stone for me. That relationship made my preference very clear.

"My husband and I divorced five years to the day after we were married, but for two-and-a-half years we were separated. It was a real battle between heterosexual orientation and homosexuality at first. It was really hard because I felt like I was straddling the fence. I felt like I really didn't belong in the women's community because I was married. I felt like I didn't belong with my husband because I really wanted to be with women. It was really difficult, also, because sometimes women didn't want to have anything to do with me because I was married, and I felt ostracized. On the other hand, a lot of the women were really friendly and made a beeline for the coming-out woman.

"It was increasingly uncomfortable for me to be married, and I started reading the books that were available. The way my husband found out was that he found these books. We worked different shifts, and I would read at night and put the books under my mattress. I would sneak the books out and take them to work with me and read them at lunch.

"Then one day I was in a hurry and I left the books out. He found the books and wanted to know what that was all about. I had been struggling with this issue of ending our marriage and trying to decide if I was really a lesbian. So, I just sat him down and said, 'Well, look! It's not working out. I really want to get a divorce. We aren't making each other happy . . . I'm really a lesbian and I need to get where I feel comfortable.' But he did so much crying that I ended up saying, 'O.K., we won't get a divorce; I'll try to work it through.'

"That lasted a year and then I just couldn't do it anymore. It finally became a battle all the time. Every time I walked out of the door he wanted to know where I was going and what I was doing. He didn't trust me and I didn't feel good about myself. I was very uncomfortable.

"I am not currently in a relationship with a woman. I've had a couple of relationships which I felt were heart connections; but to me, there are a lot of things that are really hard. A lot of us women in the community have so many family-of-origin issues. I think that keeps a lot of women from emotionally connecting. You do get involved with someone and they have so many issues to work through, it makes it really hard to have a relationship. I think it's very easy to say, 'It's too much trouble and it's too hard.'

"I haven't found many long-term relationships. That's one of my greatest disappointments in the lesbian community— although it may be a universal thing and not just within the lesbian community. I do, however, find that my friendships are so fulfilling. I'm most grateful for the friends I have made in the women's community. I am not a separatist, but, I find it better to stay in the women's community. We share so many social occasions and have many things in common. I think that that's the greatest gift I could have ever received.

"I'm out to my mother. I'm out to my two sisters and my brother, but not to my father. My sisters said they were not surprised. One sister is very loving and is just a non-judgmen-

56

tal person. She just loves me for whoever I am. The other sister thinks this is a phase. I've always had conflicts with this sister. We see the world through different eyes. My brother was very loving and just said that he wanted me to be happy.

"I didn't tell my father. My father's sister is lesbian, and she came out and left her husband to be with a woman when I was 11. She's had two partners in these years. She's my role model. My dad doesn't have a lot to do with her. He doesn't approve of it. I don't tell him because of what went on with his sister and, also, because he has leukemia. He doesn't have that long to live and it's one less stress to be between us for as long as he lives.

"My mother is a jewel. When I came out to my mom I brought her some books. When we talked, it was truly the most heart-to-heart conversation we'd ever had. I told her that I didn't want to be isolated from her and not share who I was, and that I didn't want to have to be careful with what I said to her. I didn't want a wall between us. I said, 'Mama, I'm a lot like Aunt Nell.' I think mama actually knew.

"My mother is a Christian, and her major concern was whether I might not get into heaven with her. I told her that she had instilled good morals, standards, and ethics—and through those values I'd get through the gates of heaven. It would not rest on whether I was a lesbian or not. That was a really good conversation, and then we got into whether I thought parents had any influence on kids. It was wonderful.

"Then the next day, she was really angry. It came out in ways like old history being brought up. Then, a little while later, she told me some of the family were talking about the queers, and she didn't know what to do with that. All of a sudden 'queer' became personal. It really hurt her feelings a lot. She didn't know what to do with it.

"I talked to her about it and told her she needed to share with her family so she would have someone to support her. She said she couldn't do that. I suggested her minister, and she said she couldn't share with him. That was really hard because she felt isolated. I told her I felt so much lighter having shared with her and she said, 'I'm glad you feel better; now I have to carry the burden.' She started to cry and yell more about the burden. I screamed, 'Mama, put the burden down!' There was quiet—and then I heard this little chuckle on the side. Since then she has been really close to me. I didn't play the game and allow her to guilt-trip me, and it's been a lot better between us.

"I've had a problem with both drugs and alcohol. I started smoking marijuana and drank a lot of alcohol in high school. My father's an alcoholic. When I came back to the U.S. I immediately got into the drug culture. I got really involved, really sick. I got in trouble with the law several times for selling. I was involved in a biker community for quite a few years. I couldn't really keep a job. I made most of my money through drugs.

"I got into a serious car accident and that stopped me in my tracks. I started looking at what I was doing with my life. That was late 1976. The next year was physical recovery. I decided to change geographical locations, and I decided to never do drugs again. I continued with alcohol, not realizing it was a problem.

"It will be two years in March since I've been in alcohol recovery. It's been really good. I went to Stonewall Treatment Center, which was just a godsend. I do AA meetings. It's been a real learning experience. When your head's clear, your heart's clear."

good **J. C.**

I wish I had known back in high school what I know now.
It would have saved me a whole lot of pain. I had a certain
amount of integrity in relationships, but there was border-
line promiscuity. It was like trying to fill this spot that
never got filled.

J.C. was born in 1947 in the state of Washington. She has degrees in art and music and has a lot of classes and courses accumulated since then. She teaches art and music.

"I understand a lot of women know that they are lesbians early on. But I grew up in a capsule. My father was a professor and a part of a medical community, so we had a very protected environment.

"I did very little dating while I was in high school, as I was very involved in art and music and performing. Then, when I got into college, I started dating a lot. I was always attracted to people who were very bright and, in my sophomore year, I started living with a fellow who was a physicist. Our relationship was fine as long as it was intellectual in content, but when it got down to the day-to-day living, problems came up. He said the way I responded to him after sexual activity was like I had been soiled. At that point in my life I had no idea that there was an alternative. I didn't know anybody gay—you know?

"So, I lived with him for four years. My relationships always started out with a lot of heavy sexual activity and then after a period of time it came down to nothing. That was true in this one, too, and it created a lot of conflict. Then I finally moved out of there.

"Then, after college, I was living in Seattle and I met a fellow who lived in New York. He did all those wonderful things that are taught to us in little fairy tale books. He sent flowers every three or four days. I was real impressed by that. All the women I worked with thought he was wonderful, and

I ended up marrying the guy and moving to New York. That didn't last too long because he drank a lot. I thought he was a social drinker, but actually he was an alcoholic. I was fairly isolated, too, because I didn't really know anybody there. It's interesting that he still calls on anniversaries and stuff. We didn't bury the hatchet in each other. I divorced him in the early seventies.

"Then I got into banking and banking management. That's a real neurotic occupation. I did well at it. I met a fellow there who was a lobby guard. I was engaged to him for a while and then started dating a friend of his.

"Most of my relationships had a three-month span. I dated a lot of different people because nothing very satisfactory seemed to be happening. I had dated a lot of different people and I was pretty sexually active, but as I look back on it now, I know that I had an underlying attitude of disrespect of men. I think sex was their primary focus. Relationships were very disappointing to me . . . they were lacking in depth. It was like, 'What is it that I'm supposed to be experiencing?' I wondered what everybody seemed to get so excited about. I dated men with a lot of different ethnic backgrounds and occupations.

"Finally, at 29 I thought it was time to be married and have a family. All that family pressure stuff. I was introduced to a fellow who was a widower and he had a three-and-a-half-year old daughter. I married him within six months. Then I became pregnant and, within the next year, I had another daughter. I was used to changing relationships, but now I had a real commitment to being a parent and I felt I should honor what I had started. So, I was married for seven years. He was a very controlling, abusive person and a police officer. Who better to take care of me than somebody strong and in uniform? Big lie!

"Then in 1985, my mother was dying of cancer. For the last three months of her life, she was totally bedridden. So, I took the girls with me back home and cared for my mother until she died. As her life was ending, it really made me think about the direction my life was taking. I decided that I did not want to go back to this marriage. I could see how little caring he really was capable of. I had a big awakening. I knew that I needed to do something else with my life. So I came back and I divorced him. "That was a traumatic process. He has still not made it easy after all this time. I realized that I had to make a living and support myself. I had stopped working when my daughter was born. To move away from the work force is very disabling, no matter how strong you are. I decided to make a living doing something that was more suited to who I was. It was scary but I believed in myself.

"My daughters were in a private school at the time. I started putting together my music and my art, and I was able to create the music program at that school. I did that for three years. I had free rein to just create it, and it was very successful.

"There was another private school in the area that had heard about the program; soon I was doing two private schools. During that time I started doing classes with little people— two-year-olds and a little older—music education classes. I took those kids as they grew and they became my piano students. I did some advertising and sent out fliers. At the present time, I don't have to do anything to create a full load. I have more people than I can fit into my schedule. So making an income finally took care of itself.

"I was working at this private school and I had this free hour-and-a-half on the days that I taught, because I had to give my daughter a ride home. I always went to this one particular place for lunch during that time. There was a woman working there whom I started having little short conversations with and it was really nice. All of a sudden, one day, I realized that I really looked forward to going in there and talking with her. Then it dawned on me that the reaction I was having wasn't like a lot of other friends that I've had. It was a real attraction, and I thought, 'Oh, dear!'

"When I was in college, there was a woman who lived across the hall who was lesbian, but I didn't know it then. She used to arrange dates for me with her gay male friends because I preferred men who were polite and knew how to behave appropriately. They were always a terrific date. When I moved here, I sent her a card and she came over with her roommate at the time, and it was like, "Oh—your roommate.' It never occurred to me then. That was my only contact with lesbians. When I was working at the bank, I also managed an apartment building. In the building, I had a number of tenants who were gay men, and I got along with them really well. These were my only contacts with the gay world.

"So, here I am at the restaurant saying, 'Hm . . . this is really different.' As I continued to go in there, I began to consider myself in the middle of something like a teenage infatuation. It was terrible!

"Then I had a woman who brought her daughter to me for piano lessons, and she was noticing some of these changes I was going through. I was noticing her a little bit, too! One day she brought me some music tapes and told me that she had brought me some women's music to listen to. I thought that was fine because I was a feminist. She said, 'You may want to listen to this when you're alone.' It was a tape of one of Olivia's anniversary concerts. She told me there was a concert coming up and would I be interested in going with her and another friend of hers. She had brought her roommate here a couple of times with the kids, and I kind of wondered about it.

"Finally, I started to talk with her about these feelings I was having. All of a sudden, she up and moves to New York! Always before in relationships, when I considered them over, it was no big deal. But in this case I thought somebody had ripped my insides out. I was just devastated by this.

"In the meantime, I was looking for a counselor as I felt very edgy and confused, and I talked to a friend who recommended one. It was important to me to have a counselor who was a lesbian and who had a stable relationship because I knew nothing about stable relationships. I wasn't sure that stable relationships were ever possible. Counseling has been a very positive experience for me.

"Anyway, this friend who recommended the counselor shared similar experiences with me. She said, 'There is something I want to share with you.' And then I said, 'There is something I want to tell you about, too.' As it turned out she had a crush on somebody she worked with and I had this big hot crush on this waitress. We thought that was pretty enter-taining! So, I was able to start moving through my confusion to some clarification. My friend and I ended up coming out about the same time.

"I absolutely consider myself a lesbian now. In retrospect, I can see that there were a lot of things I didn't cue into growing up—a lot of things I didn't see.

"I had a good time telling some of my friends. I really enjoyed it. It was like this great discovery that I had made. I told some very old friends of mine and I've had no backlash. They were just fine. It speaks of the quality of friendship I had established. My feeling was that if it was something they couldn't handle, then I had made an error in evaluating the things that our friendships were based on. Acceptance of differences is important to me. This one woman that I told had always kind of looked to me as the person she always wanted to be because I did a lot of dating. It took her about a week before she could talk to me again. But, she called back and said that she had had a real hard time with it. Then, she introduced me to the first woman I was physically involved with.

"My friend had said that she knew this gay fellow who had a lesbian roommate who was about my age, and that maybe we could talk together. She knew that I had lots of questions.

"I got involved in that relationship, and the woman needed a place to live because the fellow she was with was moving. We were dating at the time and she asked if she could move in, just for thirty days. I didn't know how to say no to her. I didn't want to tell her that I wasn't ready to have anyone move in with me. I had two children that I was not out to, I had all this stuff to consider and I really didn't want to make that as a choice yet. But, at the same time, I wanted to be a nice person—and so she moved in. That was two-and-half-years ago, and she is still here. During the time she's been here I have always said right up front that everything is a day at a time.

"There was one time in particular that I was just a touch involved with another woman who came along during this time, and who is still a friend of mine, in fact. I felt like I needed some more experience. I needed to know whether I was committed to this change or whether I was just fed up with the male population. Men just make me crazy.

"I find the energy with women is entirely different. I do have a real preference. There is a kind of being present in an emotional way with women. I had a lot of opportunity to experience this with men, and they just weren't there emotionally. It was more like something was done to you. You might both be participating, but there was nothing mutual about it. There were a lot of things lacking that I think are more prevalent in the nature of women. I think there are biological differences that show up in those areas.

"People say, 'Well, what can women do?' I had that question, too. I found out it is more than satisfactory for me. I would like to think that somewhere down the road there would be a relationship that is really fulfilling to me in a lot of areas. The person I've been with is very, very nice. We've had very little conflict. The problem is me—not her. I think that I need to find a relationship that works in more areas for me.

"When I was in high school, there was a young woman who was involved in music with me who discovered her sexuality at that time. I knew she was a very tactile person, and very warm, and I really liked her a lot. I realized later that I was very jealous of the fact that she was so attached to one of the women in our vocal ensemble. We were really good friends, and I really didn't like that she was so attached to her. I was her friend and I was jealous, but, at the time, I didn't identify what was going on. Now she and I are corresponding, and we see each other from time to time. Incidentally, she never married.

"I have this really scary feeling inside that at some point down the road there is a relationship that could really work out to be something of long-term value. I'm glad that it isn't right now because I have a lot of other issues that I'm working through . . . parenting stuff.

"One of my children is going to be 19 in February and has been living at home until just this last month. She has gone through a lot of rebellion, and her father has just been a phenomenal jerk during this whole period of time. I cannot be out with my children because of him. He is a raving fundamen-

64

talist—and a cop. He is a rigid, vengeful person. It would be like a big court battle and all that—not because he wants the children. The oldest child, whom I adopted, is his child from his first marriage.

"My younger daughter is 12. They are completely different. The younger one is very musical and is extremely intellectual. She is talking about the full scholarship to Stanford that she plans to have. She is a scholar, and she could pull it off. I have some feelings about watching her. I don't know what the inherited genetic programming may be. There is the potential that this child may one day come home and say 'Mom, there is something I want to tell you.' She has said that she knows she could date someone who is Jewish or black—or could even bring home a girlfriend, and not a boyfriend. She knows it would be O.K. with me if they were good persons.

"I am not out to my children. I think at some level they know. I think that their not knowing is the best, considering where my oldest daughter is right now. I would eventually like to be out to them. My family does not know about my sexuality.

"I'd like to reach a point where I can just be out, period. It's not part of my nature to be secretive, and it is extremely difficult for me. I deal with a lot of small children who belong to parents who have different attitudes than I do. It could be very impacting on my business. If I can create some income that is not from the teaching, I could do more things, one of which is to be more out. I can be more comfortable in open settings.

"It could be difficult for my kids, with all the emotional things they have had to handle. I have told them that we have friends whom we have known for a long time and whom we love and respect, and they are gay.

"I am a terrible flirt; I have no problem with that at all. I don't mind being somewhat demonstrative in public within the limits of what is appropriate for anyone. If you hang and clutch at someone, I think that makes other people uncomfortable. The thing I resent is going to a restaurant and seeing this fellow and his girlfriend holding hands. I feel cheated when I can't do the same; that hurts me inside. What ends up happening is that I choose to go to places where there are a lot of gay people. I resent the fact that I can't go just anywhere.

"I am not out to my family. I think they have a question about me because I've had this woman living with me for a couple of years now. She just sort of goes everywhere, like family. My ex-husband made some comments about it. He thought it didn't look good for me to have another adult woman living in the same house. He said to my children that maybe I was a lesbian. They came home and they were all upset about that. I told them that I was sorry that he was concerned with that, and that they know who I am and the kind of person that I am. I said that it wasn't his job to mind my business. It is hard for me. I don't want to lie to them, but I don't want to put them in a strange position.

"I would like to be living in a more isolated place. If it were overlooking the ocean that would make me happy. I would like to have a studio there. Besides my art and musical composition, I write. Eventually, I'd like to think of residuals and walking to the mailbox and finding checks.

"If I could have the kind of relationship that I really want, that would be great. I know there are going to be very few people who are going to be in that accepting, wise, intellectual, spiritual place with me. I need those things to match up.

"I have a very wide range of friends who are lesbian. I decided I needed a social circle, and I just went about collecting friends. I know a lot of really fine people, and the rate of gays and lesbians in our population is not 10 percent. It's closer to thirty! I'll bet you money on that. I've got excellent radar.

"I wish I had known back in high school what I know now. It would have saved me a whole lot of pain. I had a certain amount of integrity in relationships, but there was borderline promiscuity. It was like trying to fill this spot up that never quite got filled.

"My advice for women considering being lesbian is the sooner they check it out, the better. Husbands seem to think that the change is all about them when it really has nothing to do with them at all—the male ego thing.

"Women who are considering being lesbian need to think of the what ifs, especially with regards to children, where some caution is necessary. Kids have a tough time with it, although the age of the child makes a difference. They go through those stages when they want to be exactly like everyone else. They want that picture of the all-American average family.

"I think women should plug into some sort of support system, and I think counseling helps. I think they should go into counseling with someone who is gay or lesbian so that they don't end up with somebody who is going to try and fix what's wrong with them. If they build on what they are interested in, they will meet people everywhere they go."

Mari Ann

I didn't decide to be a lesbian; I think I just gave in to it.

Mari Ann is 28. She was born in Seattle, Washington. She is a florist.

"I was first married in 1981. I was just eighteen. I think I got married to get out of the house. I wanted to be on my own. I wanted to have a home of my own. I wanted to get on with things, and I thought that was the only way. I thought that was what you were supposed to do.

"We were married for almost five years. He was slightly older than I and had an alcohol problem. He was mentally abusive. He almost had me convinced that it was my fault that he had the drinking problem. He almost got me on that one. He was sleeping with a friend of mine, and that ended it for me. I initiated the divorce. I'm sure glad I found that out, or maybe it would have gone on longer.

"My second marriage was in 1986. I married a wonderful, kind person that I didn't know for very long. We had both gone through a lot in our first marriages and came together because we were lonely and we were a comfort to each other. We finally realized that we didn't have a whole lot in common. He was also unfaithful. I was the one who initiated that divorce also. That marriage ended in 1989. I'm still in contact with him. He's married to a nice woman. I had no children from either marriage.

"I didn't decide to be lesbian; I think I just gave in to it. I always knew that I wasn't very attracted to men. I didn't much like them, either. I still don't. I can think of a few that I think are O.K. people.

"I've always been attracted to women and finally found gay friends when I changed my job and went into the flower business. I grew up in a small suburb, a really closed-minded little area. I never knew any gay people.

"When I met these people, I thought 'That that's the lifestyle I'd like to lead.' I started reading *The Weekly*—the personals. Gosh, there were gay women who wanted to meet other women in that paper. I thought, 'Why not?'

"I answered one ad and got my mail order bride. She's wonderful. She was exactly what I would have described as my ideal. It's amazing that it happened that way. She had answered many ads herself before she put an ad in. She went on lots of dates, but darned if she didn't pick me. It just worked out so well. I've had other affairs, but I've never really been in love until her. I am monogamous.

"It felt so right to have my love interest be a woman. It was so normal. It was like I'd finally found the right thing to do.

"I came out to everybody in the world. I called my Mom and told her, and my family and my friends, and everybody at work. It felt very right.

"I was rejected by only two people. I had a good friend who was very active in her church. She and I still correspond but we are much more distant than we were, and that's kind of sad.

"My brother had a hard time with it. He didn't want to invite me to family events. He couldn't understand how I could be such a different person. This brother is 11 years older than I. This Christmas, I called and said, 'Is it just my imagination, or are we not having Christmas? Tell me what's going on.' I have always been the initiator of these family things. It turned out that nobody had done anything. At the last function, he said, 'Please come, but don't let anybody know about what you're doing.' It was O.K. for my partner to come as long as we didn't say what was going on. I told him I couldn't do that. I felt it was being untrue to myself.

"Anyway, we worked it out for Christmas, and he was almost getting used to the idea when his wife's brother told the family that in addition to being gay, he had AIDS! The whole family is in shock.

"I talked to my bother a couple of days ago, and he said that he really wasn't an Archie Bunker, and that he had begun to view things a lot differently. I said, 'Yeah, you are ... but you're doing a lot better.' They are helping the brother and supporting him.

"My mom still thinks I'm going to change my mind. The thing is, she just loves Joan, and they've accepted us. However, the other day she said, 'But you're so feminine.' I said, 'It's O.K., Mom; don't worry about it. You didn't do it.'

"My father just says, 'Don't say anything to anybody.' Everybody is so concerned about how it makes them look. My mom says, 'Don't tell our side of the family until I'm dead.' The thing is, I would like to tell those people I am close to. It would be natural to tell.

"I'm out at work. My boss is a wonderful guy. I don't think I said directly to him what was going on, but he picked it up. One day when we were alone, he said, 'I'm sure glad you got that sexuality thing worked out.' He said I was so much happier. I've been there five years. He saw me go through my divorce; he's been so supportive.

"My partner is not out at all. Her mom came to stay recently and it was real straighten-up time. Hide the newspapers and don't call her 'Honey.' Her family is all in Idaho, so it's easy to be in the old closet.

"She practices being out with my friends and family. I finally realized that's what she was doing! I have been in therapy for 17 years, and I finally realized with my shrink's help that it wasn't so much that I wanted her to tell her family. . . . I wanted her to act like she was a part of our partnership. Now she is. It's very much like we're a family. That was very important to me.

"We have been together a year and a half. Her mom may know; I think she can figure it out. Her mom and I get along very well.

"I'm thinking about changing jobs. I'm not sure exactly what I want to do. I think I'm at the nicest place I could be in the city. I might want to keep doing that for awhile, but I'm at the top of the pay scale, and, in the back of my mind, it seems like I should go to school. I'd like to be an antique dealer or even a junk store owner."

Donna

While I didn't find the initial sexual experience with my husband to be entirely repellent, it did not inspire a closer or warm relationship with the man.

Donna is 62. She was born in Houston, Texas. She has a doctoral degree and is a retired professor of nursing.

"I consider myself a lesbian—and have for almost 40 years. Since my first lesbian experience, it was crystal clear that I was a lesbian.

"Prior to that experience, I had, in my youth, dated men consistently—although I was not what you would call roaringly popular.

"At the age of 19, I was married to a man I had known for five years. He had been a ranger in World War II. All of this was very romantic and people were getting married all around. I decided that would be the best thing to do.

"I was a virgin at the time of my marriage, and if my husband had any experience, I think it was very limited. In any event, while I didn't find the initial sexual experience to be entirely repellent, it did not inspire a closer or warm relationship with the man.

"I never found the relationship fulfilling in any sense except that the state of being married offered a certain status among my friends and colleagues. I remained married for approximately a year and a half, and we eventually separated and divorced.

"I graduated from school and proceeded to another city and went to work in a hospital. There I met this senior student who would graduate in not too long, and she became my first female lover.

"My friendship with this student had all of the elements of courtship—leading up to romantic and sexual love. That included the poems that to the present day are those which are shared by lovers. There was a sensitivity to what was going on in our profession of nursing, a sensitivity and compassion, an empathy which she had for our patients, which I found warming and enveloping to share.

"We spent a great deal of time together—sharing our mealtimes at the hospital and as much time as possible off duty. I lived outside the hospital, and she lived in a dormitory room shared by two other women who were straight. She was a very beautiful young woman, had been a winner of several beauty contests and was very sought after by young men. She dated regularly.

"One day, as we lay across a bed reading a poem, our hands touched in the first physical contact. It was like a pink-backed romantic novel—I might suggest that the veil fell from our eyes. We realized the physical relationship which would follow.

"I think it was clear to us that this relationship was not acceptable, but we were very naive about keeping it hidden. Although we both continued to date men and on occasion double dated, it must have been plain to many people that our relationship was more than ordinary friendship.

"The most serious thing that happened was when I went on a vacation at the height of this romance. I wrote love letters which my lover's roommate found and delivered, as good Christian girls should, to my lover's sister. We had a confrontation in which I denied steadily that any of this was so. I said I could see how those letters could make it seem otherwise. Nothing came of the confrontation except to heighten my awareness of the unacceptability of the relationship.

"Over the years since 1947, there have been a number of times when I thought it would have been a great pleasure and a great relief to come out of the closet. I felt this most in the late sixties and early seventies when the feminist movement was strongest. But at that time I concluded that revealing my lesbianism was a luxury—a self-indulgence—which still in the eighties can put a variety of life values in jeopardy with catharsis being the only advantage. Once a thing is said it can never be taken back, and things are altered for all time. I feel as

72

if I would be ashamed in the eyes of some persons. I would be afraid that it would threaten my job security. For me, now, I don't know how much there is a real need for hiding and how much is a life-long practice.

"My family circle narrows as I grow older. I do not feel alienated from them, yet I feel that I can never be completely close because of this secret. It's part of my personality to have total openness, and here is a basic ingredient of my life about which I cannot feel open. This is especially true with my oldest sister who lives here in the same city. I feel close, and I think she knows I am gay, but we have never discussed it and I see no probability or good reason to do so.

"What do I do for fun? I play bridge. I swap video cassettes with friends. I like to play board games. I fish when I can find fishing companions, which is as much a problem as finding a sexual companion.

"The world talks of sexual preference. I know it's the only term we can use—it's a kind of generic term. But, you know, I really dislike it. It sounds as though sometime at puberty there was someone who held out two hands and said, 'Here is heterosexuality, and here is homosexuality; which do you pick?' Actually, we lesbians know that it isn't like that at all. We are as surely homosexual as straight people are heterosexual.

"I am a lesbian and that's just the way it is. I have not wished to live my life differently. I have been privileged to know and love some wonderful women, and I would not have wished to change that."

Eleanor

I felt that I had come home. It was an 'A-Ha!' experience.

Eleanor is 53. She was born in Baldwinsville, New York. She has an A.A. degree in nursery school education and works in a public school system.

"I remember when I was young that I wished I could figure out a way to have children without men.

"As long as I can remember I wanted to be a mother. I had four children in less than five years. Not so great, let me tell you! I was married two weeks after I graduated from junior college. It was in 1958, and I was twenty years old. We moved to New York City where I was teaching in a nursery school. My husband was an apprentice to become a funeral director. We lived in New York city for four years and during that time I had three babies. Seven months after we got married I got pregnant and from then on it was babies.

"My marriage was mostly raising a family. I worked very little outside of the home. My husband was an alcoholic and that was probably the biggest problem in our marriage. We were very much in love when we got married and very close, but when the alcohol started interfering with the relationship—it just started crumbling. I think I've realized that I should have left that marriage after 10 years, but I was afraid of being on my own. I didn't feel that I could do anything. I didn't feel that I could support myself and the children, and I wanted the marriage to work.

"I wanted to be married. I didn't want to be single. We had visions of all these wonderful things we were going to do when the children were grown and he was retired. I didn't want out until it got so bad that I realized that's what I had to do. That was about twenty years into the marriage. The youngest was 14 . . . 14 to 19.

"I had a problem with alcohol during the marriage, too, because I would go along with it. It got so my drinking was a daily thing. Then one day I looked at it pretty seriously, and I went to a hypnotist out of curiosity. The group he had was a group who wanted to quit smoking. When he hypnotized us, I substituted drinking for smoking. After that session I didn't drink for four years. I had no more desire. After that when I did drink it was very moderate.

"So, finally, I went to a lawyer and got a legal separation, thinking that it would straighten him out. I thought that he'd straighten out and I would go back to him. It didn't take me too long to figure out that we don't straighten people out; we can only take care of ourselves. We were separated for two years but still very married. Neither one of us dated anyone else. We would take vacations together and do things together. I had moved into an apartment with my youngest daughter. The other children chose to stay with their father. They realized that if they lived with me it was going to be a greater responsibility for them as they would have to contribute to the household.

"After two years I moved. I felt like I was in the mire—I wasn't married and I wasn't not married. I got no support from my husband except for $35-a-week child support. So I ended up working two jobs. I had a lot of anger and resentment. Between the two jobs I was working seven days a week.

"I filed for divorce about two years later. One reason I waited so long was because of his insurance. There was a certain amount of security in still being legally married. I think I was afraid of letting go completely. Then, one day, I just said, 'I'm gonna do it.'

"It was quite a few years later, actually, that I realized that I was interested in women. I didn't think I had any feelings for women. I had quite a few gay men friends. They would kid around with me saying, 'When are you going to change over?' Even some younger female friends came right out and asked me, 'Are you lesbian?' And I'd say, 'Well, I don't think I am.'

"I was confused, I really was. I still had some interest in men. I dated a little bit, but not very much. I can't say that I really enjoyed it that much. I realized that my friends were all women or gay men. I really never had friendships with heterosexual men.

"Then, it finally happened about four years ago. I was working in a restaurant where one of the owners was gay, and he knew that I was leaning towards women. Some people were having a birthday party, and everyone who worked at the restaurant was invited to the party. My oldest daughter was working with me at the time. When we got to the party, there was a young woman there named June. She was the lover of the daughter of one of my closest friends. I happened to know her, and as the party was progressing, one of the guys said to me, 'June is in love with you.' I said, 'I have known June for 10 years. She loves me and I love her, but she is young enough to be my daughter.'

"I really didn't think any more about it. Then she just kind of started coming on to me, but she had been drinking. I was sitting in a chair, and she came over and sat in my lap and put her arms around me. Then she asked me if I would go out to lunch with her sometime and I said sure.

"I was living with a woman at the time; it was a platonic friendship. But she asked me, 'When are you going to call June and have lunch with her.' I said, 'I will get around to it one of these days.' I finally did call her and then we got together. It really didn't last very long because every time we started getting close she would run away. She was scared to death of the whole thing. But that was my initiation.

"I felt that I had come home. It was an 'A-Ha!' experience. I wanted to put it in the *Chronicle* or the *Post*. I called a local TV station which aired women's stuff and told them I had just come home. I called my ex-husband and told him. He told me that he wasn't surprised, that he had felt that from me for a long time because of my friends. I hung around a lot of women who were closeted lesbians. I was attracted to them and he knew it.

"Now I am with Pat. When we got together, we just knew that we were supposed to be together. After the first night we spent together, there were probably two nights we didn't spend together. Our first date was in November 1990 and we moved in together in January 1991. I met her at a group of lesbians over the age of fifty; the meeting was held in a church. Now, I tell people I met her at church. She just cracks up. It was my second meeting with the group; I'm very glad I went.

"I am out to my kids. When I told my oldest daughter, Sandy, it was as if she had opened up the door for that conversation to come through.

"I went over to her apartment after work one night, and I was very nervous. I thought how am I going to say this and then she just said, 'How can I help you, Mom?' She said, 'Now, Mom. We've got to find a man for you.' And I said, 'Sandy, I need to tell you something.' 'You don't want a man do you? You want a woman,' she said. She was at that birthday party and she knew something about what was going on there. I told her that was true, and that I am very attracted to June. She said, 'I've known about this for a long time.' I asked, 'How long?' and she said, 'About 15 years.'

"At that time, when she was about 13 years old, I had befriended a young woman. She was about 21. Her younger brother was working for me and I met her through him. Now I had this husband who was falling out drunk by 10 o'clock at night. He wasn't a violent drunk. He just drank until he dropped.

"So, from 10 o'clock I was free to do what I wanted. She and I got very close. I never had any sexual feelings for her—I guess I suppressed them. I remember that whenever I would see her, I would just light up. We would go out and ride bikes in the summer time 'until two o'clock in the morning. I had a lot of energy, too, the kind we get when we fall in love. I could be up late and get up in the morning and be a mother.

"This was what my daughter was referring to while I was coming out to her. It seemed at the time that Sandy was O.K. about my change in lifestyle. She hugged me and said, 'Mom, I'm real happy for you.' But, as things went on, she changed. At this point, she does not speak to me. She has since become religious and she does not accept my sexual preference now. Her feeling is that I have replaced her father with a woman.

"My youngest daughter was a little bit surprised when I told her but seemed to be accepting of it. She has always been very close to me. She did go through a period when Pat and I first got together when she felt that she was losing me to this other person. She was very jealous.

"We talked about it a lot. She tried her darnedest to be as nasty to Pat as she could. She would say to me, 'Mom, do you have to spent every night with her?' I told her that I chose to. It was hard for her, but still, there was a certain level of acceptance from the beginning. On the other hand, she was very closeted about it as far as telling other people. God forbid that her boyfriend should find out.

"I have a son who lives in New York with his father, and I told him a year later. I was waiting to tell him in person, but when Pat and I moved in together last January, I called him on the phone. I really thought there would be problems, but he just said, 'Well, Mom that's all right. You're still the same person and I still love you.' He's 28. Pat and I went up to New York this past summer, and he met her. It was like he had known her all of his life.

"We took him out to dinner, and he started asking her questions about college. And we met his fiancé, who was also fine about it. She has a son who calls me 'Gramma'. He kept asking me if Pat was my friend, and I said, 'Yes, she's my best friend.' As a matter of fact, this past Christmas they came down here and stayed with us.

"I am not out in my new job. I don't know yet whether or not my job would really be threatened or not if I came out. It is difficult for me not being out. I don't understand how people manage not being out. I was out where I worked before—in the restaurant.

"My advice for women who are contemplating a change in their sexual orientation is to go for it! Some people suppress their desires consciously; but, for me, it was not a conscious thing. If you want to do it, go for it. If you feel you need counseling, go for that, too. Do whatever you need to do to make that transition."

Sarah

My advice for women who are in a marriage and thinking about getting out, is GET OUT! Just do it. It isn't that hard to meet other lesbians.

Sarah is 42. She was born in Washington, D.C. She has an A.A. degree in English. She is now studying accounting.

"When I was 16, I ran away from home to New York where I lived with gay men. There were a lot of runaway girls that lived with gay men; it was a cover for us, and they protected us. They fed us, they clothed us, they kept us off the street. They were wonderful.

"I was there about two years, and then I got very, very ill, and my parents, who were Christian Scientists, got hold of me again. They told me that I had two choices: I could marry this nice boy they had picked out for me or I could go out to St. Elizabeth's for a while. People had the power to do that to you in those days.

"I had slept with girls, but I had never identified with women. We were very careful to sleep with one boy every six months, to keep a bisexual label to it. I did a lot of drugs, and I was really in bad shape.

"I just didn't have any resistance to my parents or their plan, and he was all right. So, I was first married in 1968 when I was 19.

"We went immediately to the Orient. He was in the service, and we would see each other every six months; it was great. I had a woman I was sleeping with when I was there, and it was marvelous.

"Then, when we came back here, people expected us to be married, including our parents. It was just horrible and the marriage started coming apart. We had only slept together maybe three times when we were married; we didn't even know each other. But, now, there were all of those pressures to

79

conform to and to have kids. It got really nasty and we got to hate each other.

"So, we finally just stopped. That was in the mid-seventies. I tried to join women's groups, but they were all heterosexual, and they didn't help much.

"My second husband was a man who worked with me and he was kind and gentle. I thought then that I wasn't really gay, but I had just been married to the wrong man the first time. This man and I had been very good friends at work for a long time. I thought that he was going to deep-six my lesbianism, and it was all going to be all right.

"After we married, we got along together and had fun and we really loved each other, but sex was a terrible thing. He tried to influence me emotionally, to make me feel that I couldn't make it on my own. I worked off and on during my marriage, so that didn't always carry much weight. Then, when that didn't work, he would say that it would destroy him if I left.

"As time went on, and things got worse, I got very depressed, and, as a result, I stayed at home a lot. Every time I met a woman I liked, I'd run back in the house again. This just seemed like it was going on forever, and then I started getting physically sick.

"Finally, after the fourth minor operation in a row, a gay friend brought me the book *Another Mother Tongue*, and just said, 'Read it.' I read it, and it was the first time I could say, 'Oh, this is O.K.' But that's as far as it went. I was scared to death. I started insisting to my husband that we go out, and we went to the gay male bars. He was really good about it, as he didn't have any problem with gay men. I went to all the gay bars, but it was different this time. I was trying to find connections.

"I didn't much like the gay men anymore. I felt that the more I was trying to come out, the less supportive they were. I gave support to the guys when they were coming out for years, but when I was trying to come out they said, 'How can you do this to your husband?' They were so horrible! They told me that I couldn't possibly be a lesbian—and all this ridiculous stuff.

"Then I started going to this woman's bookstore across the bay. I'd sneak into the lending library section, and if anyone would come in, I'd throw down the book! I couldn't bring any of them into the house. This went on for about three months. Then, I got to thinking, 'Now where do you meet lesbians?' The boys were no help. I thought I should go to an organization who works for women. So I went to work for National Action Against Rape.

"You should have seen me the first night. I had hair down to my waist, and my make-up was perfect, and I had little suede booties—right? Everyone there was lesbian and wore lumberjack shirts and hiking boots. It was the perfect place to be . . . very militant women. This was in 1984, and there were still a lot of militant lesbians around. This was the heart of political lesbian land.

"At this point, I was afraid of hurting my husband. I loved him a lot, and we had been together a long time. If any of the women tried to touch me, it was all over. A couple of my lesbian friends had to literally drag me into Amelia's—a lesbian bar—I was so afraid.

"I finally signed up for a poetry class, and the women I met there had been out since the fifties. They were not very supportive, and it was a pretty hostile environment. However, one of the women there was my age. She was Israeli and had just gotten a divorce—and really knew. She was like my hero; I followed her everywhere.

"She was the one who finally got me into bars. She used to go out with my husband and me, and she would stand up to him. She was incredible. Slowly but surely, I was crawling along. One night, they dared me to go to Amelia's alone. For one thing, it was in a scary district of town. I had never gone to the grocery store without my husband at night. Anyway, I went to the bar and met this wonderful woman. We danced together and she drove me home and kissed me goodnight in front of my husband's door. She also understood that I was in no way ready for anything else.

"It turned out she had a long-term lover. I began going to their house a lot, and they double-dated with my husband and me. They helped me to get up enough nerve to walk out the door. My husband was getting very angry—and very violent. If I had gotten interested in a guy, it would have been much better. His next illusion was that we could do a menage-a-trois with one of the women I knew. When he got violent the second time, I threw what I could into a plastic bag and walked out of the door and I never came back. That was 1985.

"At this point, I was working again and was making real money. I got a little apartment of my own, for the first time in my life. I signed up at City College in the Gay and Lesbian Studies division, and I got interested in writing. In the meantime, I was seeing too much of my best friends. They were having a lot of problems, and one of them and I became very close. She was coming over to the city to stay with me. One thing led to another and . . . we both felt just terrible.

"The day after this happened, we were all supposed to go to the parade together. We couldn't keep our hands off each other, and the other woman picked up on this. It was really miserable. Finally, these two good friends stopped speaking to me. My Israeli friend had left the country, and my husband— who wielded a lot of power—was making life miserable for me.

"Eventually, my friends (I had had the affair with one of them) decided the solution was for the three of us to sleep together. We went through that thing for three months. It turned out to be very healing for their relationship—and very destructive for me. I stopped meeting other people and going anywhere where I was likely to meet other women.

"Then I wrote letters to a teacher at City College. He encouraged me to write. We would write back and forth and it was like therapy for me. It got me started writing and I ended up writing a novel! I got into a lesbian relationships group, which also helped a lot. It helped me to sort through what I wanted. It helped me think about what it meant to be a lesbian. I cut off all my hair and got with the flannel shirts.

"At that point, I stopped sleeping with men, and I went through a series of different women. I really didn't want to get very involved again. A year later, I went to class and Betty showed up, sitting next to me. She had just moved to San Francisco, and I was living in a collective at that point and we had an extra room. I talked to the women who ran the place, and that was fine; Betty moved in.

"We were friends first, and little by little, things evolved. I was very afraid of commitment. The first couple of years we were together, we didn't declare monogamy; we gave each other a lot of space. Finally, we gave up other women, and now we have been together six years.

"We are very much married. We have done all the legal paper-work that makes us as married as you can get. We own the house together. We started light and let it develop. Neither of us had had a serious lesbian relationship before.

"I had a terrible relationship with my parents, especially with my mom. There was so much bad stuff they had me in a Christian Science nursing home for awhile. My bad relationship with Mom has very little to do with my sexuality—just childhood bad stuff. I have one brother, but I haven't seen him since I was a teenager.

"I just moved to this city eight months ago, but I'm out to everyone. I have had work done on the house, and I hire only lesbians or gays to work on it. We've been doing activities where we meet other lesbians. I don't go to the bars because I have a problem with smoke. I have a very serious heart problem for which I had surgery a year ago. I think a lot of my physical problems stemmed from the early drug abuse.

"I am pretty happy the way I am. I am studying accounting, because I want to get a good job in that field. I'd love to get my book published. We are very happy; I hope that we'll be together forever.

"My advice for women who are in a marriage, and thinking about getting out, is GET OUT. Just do it. It isn't that hard to meet lesbian women. Don't put your husband through a long ordeal. You're probably doing him a big favor by freeing him to be with somebody who really wants him.

"You should do it as early as you possibly can."

Eve

It was a huge relief to change my sexual orientation. It wasn't a change, it was a discovery!

Eve is 30 years old and was born in Midland, Michigan. She has a bachelor's degree in art and completed midwifery school. She has a private practice delivering babies and doing pre-natal care.

"I moved in with John when I was 16 years old. I was with him for eight years. We didn't actually get married until I was 18. We moved in together with a really strong commitment and the intention to be married. My mother had a fit because she didn't want me to marry him. The moving in didn't thrill her, but her concern was that I not marry him. She's pretty liberal, but it was hard on her that I moved out of her home.

"It was an O.K. marriage in lots of ways, but not a terrific one. We had an ongoing discrepancy about what the word 'love' meant. He didn't want to tell me that he loved me and said it was because he wasn't head-over-heels crazy about me all the time. I claimed that nobody ever is. You have disagreements and stuff. It took me eight years to get to this conversation where I would say, 'Do you love me?' and he would say, 'Yes' and I would say, 'Yes what?' and he would say, 'I do.' Finally, I would get him to say 'I love you' altogether.

"The other big issue for me in the marriage was feminism. I was a feminist and my mother was a feminist. She had always told me to have money of my own and to take care of myself in the ways of education and a separate bank account and things like that. He didn't mind that stuff. I suppose that's why I was with him. He was fairly progressive, but not really progressive enough for me. We had a lot of fights about who would do the dishes.

"The dishes thing sort of culminated with a very sincere conversation we had one night where I was trying for the millionth time to reach some kind of compromise. Finally he said, 'When I come home from work, I just want to sit and space out for awhile because I've had a hard day. And then I want to eat, so I don't really want to cook. Then after dinner, frankly, I have better things to do.' I was speechless and I looked at him and told him that I had better things to do, too. Anyway, I took money from our joint checking account and bought a dishwasher.

"That was the story of my marriage. It was about housework. At that time, I was a full-time student working on my art degree and, at times, I was up nights doing labor support for women who were giving birth. I was busy, too. I did more than half of the work, and I also lived in an absolute pigsty for a long period of time out of pure stubbornness because I was damned if I was going to do more than half.

"Another issue in our marriage was fat phobia. At the time I first was with John, I was not particularly fat; however, I got fatter and fatter during the course of our marriage. My weight fluctuated a lot at that time. At any rate, he was never satisfied with my body. He never thought it was small enough. He always had criticism about the food I chose to eat, and yet he ate like a pig! He was thin as a rail all the time.

"Anyhow, this was a big deal for us. He would say that he wasn't attracted to me because I was too fat. At the end of our relationship he actually said that he had never been attracted to me because I was too fat. At that point, I kicked him out. That was an issue in my marriage, no matter what I weighed.

"Sex became an issue, too, for us. We did have a good sex life for quite a long time. Eventually it kind of faded out, and we had sex once a month—which wasn't close to enough for me. I always felt like a tramp because I wanted to have sex and he didn't. It was compounded by the fact that I didn't feel that he was attracted to me, and it turned out that I had reason to think that.

"On the bright side of the marriage, he let me do my own thing. He didn't hassle me. I could have friends of the sort that I wanted, and that was O.K. He was an inventor, and what he really liked to do was to come home and go down to the basement and make stuff. I liked to go to my friend's house and go dancing and things like that. He didn't have a problem with that. I pretty much had my own life.

"I carried on a couple of flirtations during the course of our relationship. We had a non-monagamy agreement in that we'd have to ask each other first. I broke that agreement to be with a woman. I was seventeen and in college—my freshman year. I went to an out-of-state college even though it meant living away from John.

"My brother was friends with this woman, and she came over to visit, and she and I pretty much fell in love at first sight. I thought she had the most beautiful hands in the world. I didn't know what I was feeling or what I was doing or anything. I just knew that I thought she was the best. We got to know each other gradually and wrote love letters to each other. She came over and visited me sometimes. It didn't really feel like a romance to me but I do remember having a big, big crush on her.

"One day, she came to the school where I was and told me that she had dropped out of school and was going home, that her parents needed her. She asked if I wanted to come along from Indiana to Colorado. So I said, 'Sure.'

"I took homework with me and we read *King Lear* in the car. The plan was that we were going to drive to Colorado, she was going to drive me back to school for my finals, and then drive back to Colorado. Don't ask me why we didn't just do a road trip to someplace other than Colorado. I don't know.

"Anyway, on the trip to Colorado, we identified what we were doing as love—not as lesbianism. Sue was one year older than I was. I do think she was a little more on top of the lesbian issue, although she was not out at that time. So we took this trip, and we slept in the same bed, and there was all this sexual tension. After awhile the car broke down and her parents wouldn't help us. We ended up calling my mom, and she bought us both plane tickets back to Indiana so I could be there for my finals. Sue and I spent finals week back in my dorm room and we spent a lot of time hugging and kissing.

"At some point in there, it dawned on me that I had told John I wouldn't do that. I was sorry about it and was somewhat guilt-ridden—but not guilt-ridden enough to stop kissing her. I did confess over the telephone, though. He said that he suspected as much. He wasn't too upset about it until he came to where I was, and he told me that I had to choose between the two of them. It was clear that I would choose him as I had this established relationship with him. I barely knew her, and she was doing different stuff with her life.

"I transferred schools to where I could be with John. Sue came to visit and went to classes with me. It seemed like we couldn't be together without being hot for each other. I guess this is reasonable when you think about thwarted love at 17. Anyway, there we were.

"She got involved with a woman shortly after that for a couple of years, and then with another woman for a couple of years after that. I got married, and Sue was the maid of honor at my wedding. That is something I'm not particularly proud of. She'd come to visit me every year or so all during the years of my marriage. We discovered that we didn't have much to talk about, but we were intensely attracted to one another. We would be reminiscing and talking and laughing and all of a sudden there would be all this sexual tension.

"It wasn't like I was trying to be so true to John, but more that I was trying to stay out of a relationship with Sue. I did not even consider the issue of lesbianism. By then, Sue had come out as a lesbian, so I had heard the word and I knew the concept. She and I had talked about it and I knew it was in the air.

"I knew I had been in love with her. I had sort of forgotten the significance of that somewhere along the line. I'm a great one at forgetting significant events. I knew we had kissed and all that stuff, but I didn't really remember that we had been in love.

"Anyway, years later, we were having a phone conversation and I told her that I was moving to another city to go to mid-wifery school. She thought that was a great idea, that I was moving and leaving John. I moved to where I didn't know a soul and got involved right away with the lesbian community, and a few weeks later I came out as a lesbian! Sue sent me a dozen roses for a housewarming and a coming-out gift. That was October—and darned if she wasn't there at Halloween! "We weren't together for more than three hours before we were in bed together. After all those years, Sue was my first woman lover. I actually came out a couple of months before I slept with her. This relationship with Sue has gone on and off for 12 years. She and I were sexually involved for a few months, and then we broke up.

"My coming out happened like this. I had only been in this city a few weeks. I had gotten away from everything—my mother, my husband, my family, my friends and all my support group. I had never been in a situation like this before where I was completely independent and completely alone. I was staying at the house of a couple of lesbians. I am a Quaker, and I had attended some meetings and asked if anyone had some housing; these two women had offered to let me stay there for a couple of weeks. I was enamored with the idea of lesbianism, but I couldn't be a lesbian because I thought I wasn't attracted to women. I had forgotten all the women that I had been attracted to in my life. I had even forgotten that Sue and I had been in love. I had forgotten all this stuff, and here I was in this lesbian household with no ties to my old reality at all.

"This is kind of embarrassing to admit, but my husband had made such a big deal about how hard it was for me to achieve orgasm and how weird he thought that was. It's just absurd because it's not that hard and it's not that weird, but it was a big deal for him. So, of course, I had thought that it was really hard to have sex with a woman and have her have an orgasm.

"First of all, I had an unrealistic idea of how important it was for her to have an orgasm. But, then, I had this incredible idea that I couldn't bring a woman to orgasm, therefore I couldn't be a lesbian. I had this idea that if I left all my friends and went to this city where I knew there were lots of lesbians that I could just not tell anybody that I wasn't a lesbian. I could just never have any relationships but I could be a lesbian. That was my plan—I was going to be an incognito dyke.

"As a part of my feminism when I was married, I wanted so badly to be a lesbian but didn't think I could be because I wasn't attracted to women. I wanted to be a lesbian because I loved women and I completely identified with women. All my friends were women; I had lots of lesbian friends.

"Here, I didn't have the old ties. I regained a lot of memory and it was a wild, wild ride. I remembered going to bed with a girl when I was eight years old and we had this sexual relationship. We had it for a couple of years and we were orgasmic. I decided that if I could do this when I was eight, I could do it now!

"So, I sat down to dinner with the women I was staying with and told them I was confused. They asked me what I was confused about and I told them I was really confused about my sexuality. They had checked me out from the minute I came in their door and had been waiting for this conversation. They said it sounded like I was a lesbian and a part of me went, 'Yeah—All Right!' And another part wondered what that really meant to me. They suggested that I go to the lesbian center and get in a group. I went to a Lesbians-in-Transition group. I felt like I had been coming out for the last four years. I discovered I was just happy to be a dyke. In my group I met a couple of women I really liked and they are friends to this day.

"I just started coming out to people. Some of my classmates are born-again-Christians, so that was quite an ordeal. I just came out in a big, big way, and I did it before I had sex with a woman.

"It was a huge relief to change my sexual orientation. It wasn't a change; it was a discovery! It was good. When I changed my sexual orientation I saw a lot of privileges slip away . . . things like not being able to hold hands or kiss in public and like getting married. It was always kind of a cover for me to have a husband. I could do anything I wanted.

"I have had a couple more relationships with women since Sue. All my female relationships beat my marriage. One of my relationships lasted for two years. It occurred while I was in midwifery school. We challenged each other a lot in that relationship, and it was very growth producing for me. She was just out of a 10-year marriage and I was her first lesbian lover. That was a major relationship in my life. That woman is now my closest friend. I had a brief affair with another woman, and then I went through a celibacy period—not because I wanted to be single, but because I wanted to be alone. That was good for me. I did a lot of emotional healing and took care of a lot of childhood stuff.

"After that I moved to a more rural location. Out here in the boondocks, it's not that easy to participate in a same-sex relationship. I was alone for eight months in the country and got lonesome. So, I got a housemate and, while it was never our intention to become lovers, that's what happened. That's been going now for a year. No relationship is perfect, but this is very good. We are able to talk and affect change. It feels like a very successful relationship to me. It's the best relationship I've had.

"I consider myself out. I don't announce it, but, even here in the country, I would answer truthfully if I were asked. I don't talk about my personal life with my clients. I just take care of their healthcare needs. I am out to my co-workers even here in the country. I don't hold hands with my lover on the streets.

"My husband knows, my parents know and my sisters know. I have no children. I have not come out to my boss. When I told my husband, he said it was about time and he wasn't surprised. He didn't see me as any different person. At the end of my marriage, I had an affair with a man, and he also knows. He was not too thrilled that I had confided in him about my lesbian concerns. He didn't see why that should change anything in our relationship.

"I told my mom, and she burst into tears. She told me that it broke her heart that I always had to do things the hard way. She was broken-hearted to think that people would ridicule me on the streets. She said that homophobia was a real thing. She wasn't delighted, but she wasn't horrified either. My father died when I was six, and my step-father was present at this conversation. He has never said anything to me about it.

Now Mom is a great advocate of gay rights. She has marched in a parade with me.

"My parents just met my current partner six months ago. They liked her a lot. She is younger than I am and they thought it was great that I wasn't involved with someone older.

"Five years from now I want to settle down and have a baby. My health is fine. I have an ulcer but it's not active. I have a stressful life, but not because I'm a lesbian. It's related to being a healthcare provider. I want to build a house with my own hands. I want to have a stable job in a place I like living.

"Such a small part of being a lesbian is having sex with women. It is more about a feminist belief system. It's a life orientation, not just a sexual one. The single thing that kept me from coming out for the longest time was the fear of lesbian sex. I can't believe I'm the only woman in the world that has that issue. My advice is to say it's not that hard. Sex with women is much more interesting because there's much more give and take. There is much more intimacy. Having sex with a man for me was fun, but it was not nearly as much fun as with a woman because I wasn't that involved. It is possible to have sex with a man without ever doing anything.

"You just have to follow your heart. Lots of women are afraid to come out because they are afraid they'll be ridiculed or they're going to be shunned by their families. Not coming out is not going to prevent you from becoming a lesbian. You have to be who you are."

Jean

I feel that I made the right choice. It feels very solid. Now, the thought of living with a man is alien to me. Men are a different species. I know that many same-sex relationships are difficult, but it seems to me that being with the opposite sex adds another dimension of difficulty.

Jean is 45. She has a master's degree in counseling. She works part-time as a mental health counselor at a mental health agency and part-time in private practice.

"My first marriage was in 1966 and I was 20 years old. I was just a child, and so was he. It lasted four and a half years and was very difficult.

"I think we each came from two dysfunctional families and had no concept of what it was like to live with another person. We had no skills in communication. I was so blocked up with my family's lack of openness about sexuality that we couldn't even consummate the marriage in the beginning. There was no affection or warmth shared in my family. I didn't know what it was like to be affectionate or sexual with a person. Sexual things were difficult throughout the marriage. Anyway, I put him through a seminary, and then we split up, and I got a divorce in 1970.

"I married again in 1974. The biological clock was ticking and I married because I wanted to have children. I met my husband while I was a teller at a bank, and there was this very cute person with little twinkly eyes. He was adorable.

"That marriage lasted nine years. Our son, Nile, was born in 1978, and we divorced in 1981. He was from Mexico, a different culture and very rigid. He had a set view of what women did. I learned that he didn't like me when I was myself, and that was a very big lesson. I wondered what I doing in a relationship when I was not encouraged to be who I was. What I was supposed to do was to support him and, literally, take care of him. I was a housewife and a mother at that time, but I also had my own business in tiles and I was being the book-keeper for his insulation business. I was doing a lot.

"When our child was tiny, my husband was a good father; but as the child got older, we had some big conflicts in parenting. He didn't want to set limits or give the child responsibility, and I wanted to be consistent. That was a real clash on top of our already strained relationship. I finally told my husband that we needed some changes and asked him to go to counseling with me. He said, and I can almost quote it, 'There will be no changes, and I will not go to counseling.' The next week I told him there would be a divorce.

"After I had filed for divorce, Nile became ill. He was ill before we realized it, and, by the time his illness was evident, he had a stroke because of blood clots forming in the heart. He died when he was four and a half.

"After Nile's death and the divorce, I worked for awhile and then got into school. I changed my major from art to psychology, finished my B.A. and started looking for a graduate school. I needed a very strong focus because I didn't feel like living. I wanted to go back into psychology because I really liked it and, in counseling, I felt I could offer something of my experience to parents who lose children. There wasn't a lot of help back then; that was in 1982.

"During my first marriage, I had met a woman named Judith and we became very good friends. A couple of years after we met she told me that she had had a sexy dream about me. I was just horrified! It never crossed my mind. I sort of pushed her away. At that time I didn't want her to touch me. It was really scary. I thought I was plugging along as a confirmed heterosexual, but Judith prompted me to begin my introspection.

"In the beginning, I was worried about my sexuality. But as I worked through it, I didn't feel bad about it anymore and came to see it as a gift. By then, 10 years later, I thought I was bi-sexual and that felt natural. Then I thought, 'This is wonderful!' I was still married while I was working through all that.

Judith and I shared those feelings through the years and still do.

"In 1986, I was going with a man, and I might have married him . . . but then I met a woman who I got a definite crush on. I told the man about my ambivalence, and a year later the relationship with him ended and I became involved with this woman. That was my first relationship with a woman. I think I was still working through my family-of-origin issues with her, and so was she, because it was a very difficult relationship. I was with her a year and a half.

"Randi and I have been together over a year now. It feels great! I feel pretty committed to our relationship. I match her on levels I hadn't matched before. It's about spirituality and our feelings about personal growth, and our goals and our values. These are important. We really are friends. I feel really comfortable with her, and she has converted me. I am a lesbian now; I wasn't before.

"My mother is living, and she knows about my lesbianism. She lives a few hours from here in a small town. Her reaction was, 'Oh my God!'

"I am out at work and pretty much to everybody. I do have a couple of friends who I haven't talked to in a few years. A lot of my relatives don't know. I have two brothers and they know. One is being supportive now, but in the beginning he was horrified. The other brother was supportive at first and now he is horrified, so it balanced out! My oldest brother met Randi at Christmas time. I have no plans yet for having the other brother meet her.

"I feel that I made the right choice. It feels very solid. Now the thought of living with a man is alien to me. Men are a different species. I know that many same-sex relationships are difficult, but it seems to me that being with the opposite sex adds another dimension of difficulty.

"In the years to come, I hope my private practice will grow. Randi and I have an idea of forming a center for therapy and movement therapy as it relates to self-defense. It would be for women, and I see it as part of taking back our power that we've given up to men. I see it helping us to defend ourselves. It has been really hard for me to learn to use my body to defend myself.

"My advice to women who are thinking of leaving a marriage and are questioning their sexual preference would be to get a supportive female therapist, and then find supportive people. Then, give yourself time to work through it. Be kind to yourself. Go find books. I met Randi in Tae Kwon Do, and I certainly didn't expect to find her there!"

Randi

When I recognized my lesbianism, it felt like a liberation. It felt great! It was the natural thing. I'm out to everyone.

Randi is 39. She was born in Galveston, Texas. She has a certificate in automotive repair and an A.A. degree in industrial machining—a pre-engineering degree. Randi is working as an engineering technician. She is in the process of applying to a university to study psychology.

"I was married right out of high school. It was really wild. I came from a very abusive father and a chaotic family life, and all I could see was getting the hell out of the house.

"I met this guy . . . we had a kind of camaraderie. At that point, that was all I could understand. I didn't know there was anything more to it than that. As soon as I turned 18, I'd had it with living at home and I moved in with him.

"We never had a marriage ceremony; in Texas, there is common-law marriage. I found out what the rules were and started using his name. I wanted his name because I could go into the honky-tonks that way. I had aspirations of being a musician in those days. He played music, I played music, and we played together in some of the bars.

"We lived together for several years. But after about six months, I wanted out of Texas. I told him that I wanted to go to Colorado. I'd seen pictures, I'd heard about it, and I wanted to go. He was very reluctant.

"The marriage was kind of weird. I was the boss of things. He couldn't keep a job; he was very unstable. He was a good musician, but just really flakey. I kept pressuring him to go, and finally I came home with a '46 Chevy panel truck. I picked it up for $250, and said, 'I'm goin,' Baby. You can come with me, or not.' He said, 'O.K., O.K.,' and we just took off for Denver. I was only there for three weeks when I realized I hated it. I the snow. So, we got a place in the mountains above Boulder. I was just happy as hell.

"Within no time, I knew that I didn't need this marriage to get along. It was kind of a security thing, and I had had no experience of being alone. I didn't know any girls my age who would take off like that. I was pretty functional, but he was pretty dysfunctional. As soon as I had my feet on the ground, I started drifting away. He was really jealous and had fits about it all.

"We lived in a hippie-type community. This was about 1971–72. There were cabins, and we would go to each other's cabins at night, playing music and smoking pot. I didn't know a whole lot of people up there.

"One night my truck died and I hitch-hiked down to Boulder to play some music and make some money, and it started snowing. I thought, 'Oh shit, I better leave.' So, I started hitchin' home, and this guy in an old pickup picked me up. We were going up the mountain, and it was really snowing, and he was trying to make small talk. It was really a blizzard. As we were going along, all of a sudden I saw this woman. She had long blond hair sticking out of her ski cap. She put up her thumb and I yelled, 'Pull over.'

"I didn't know her or anything, but as soon as I opened the door, this light went on in my head. It was like instant recognition. She looked at me and said, 'Thanks for pulling over,' and I said, 'Thank him; it's his truck.' She figured out that I was hitchin', too.

"As we drove on, we found out that we were both heading for the same neighborhood. We found out that we both played music and that we both lived in the same rural community. So, we agreed that we'd get together soon—and that's how I met her.

"That was my first lesbian experience. It turned out that she wasn't even a lesbian. She had just come out of a relationship with a guy and had never been with a woman before. It was kind of like love at first sight for both of us. I was 19 then. It was really wild.

"It turned out that she was pretty much bi-sexual. I was the spark; I was the one who instigated the sex and stuff. You could tell she was really interested but not into the whole idea. We never lived together; she was a real traveler. She had a chance to crew on a boat, and she took off to Fiji. She was gone for awhile, and when she came back, we were together. Next, she took off for New Zealand. That was the way it went.

"In the meantime, I realized I was really into this. That's where my head was. I started finding women . . . going to the lesbian bar. I've had probably four long-term relationships.

"When I met the woman traveler, I decided I wanted my name back. I wanted away from him, so I lived in a tent for three months. I was given a bad time about that because we were considered married. I had to go get a legal divorce. I did it through legal aid, and it cost me $100. He met a woman about then and moved to New Hampshire for a year with her. I went to Europe for a year with a friend of mine.

"Then I met this woman, Laura. We were more like a partnership than a relationship. There was very little sex, but we were just really good friends and we lived together really well. We decided we were both ready to leave Colorado; that was in 1979. We bought a station wagon. I had a dog and she had four cats. We got a trailer, and we moved to Seattle together. I was with her for another couple of years.

"The thing is that ever since I was really little all my crushes were on my girlfriends. I never really understood that. No one did. When girls started dating the boys, I wanted to go with girls. When we were about 14 and going to these dances, I wanted to dance with the girls. When girls were going steady with boys, I wasn't interested. If a girl decided she didn't want to be my friend anymore, that would break my heart. All through high school I would make really close relationships with my girl friends.

"When I was 16, I had this really close friendship with Stephanie, and we spent the night together; we would just hold each other. I just loved it. We got in trouble together; we did something wild, and her parents decided I was the bad influence. They banned her from me and I cried for a week.

"When I recognized my lesbianism, it felt like a liberation. It felt great. It was the natural thing. I'm out with everyone.

"My parents were divorced when I came out. My mother's first reaction was, 'I don't need to know that! Just do what you have to do and don't give me any details!' I didn't even bother telling my dad; I knew she would. They still see each other from time to time.

"Mom has totally adjusted now. She had started college before she met my father, then bam bam bam . . . six kids. Twenty years later, she wanted to go back to school. So, she divorced him, and finally got her master's degree. She is an art therapist. She subscribes to a lot of women's magazines, and has come quite a ways. She is now able to deal with my lesbianism, and I feel she accepts me as I am.

"There were three boys and three girls in my family. They all know. I am number three in the group of six. Only my oldest sister and I are on speaking terms and we have a very good relationship. She is a psych major and teaches women's studies at a university. She has always been very liberal minded. My sexuality doesn't phase her a bit.

"The rest don't like me because I'm a lesbian. My youngest sister was a Catholic and has now turned Baptist. I can't even sleep in her house. The other brothers and sisters think I'm really sick.

"I had no children. I had a four-year relationship with a woman who had a nine-year-old boy, so I was sort of the father figure for a while.

"I smoked pot from the time I was 13 until three years ago. I was pretty much addicted to pot. I dabbled in coke, but it was too expensive for my budget. My husband was a pothead; it just became a way of life. I had an awful time getting off pot. I think pot is physically and psychologically addicting.

"I've had my current relationship for a year, and it's wonderful. It's the best part of my life. Living with Jean is like a gift.

"For fun I take and teach martial arts. Karate is my main interest. I do it three or four times a week.

"In 10 years, I want to get at least a B.A. in psychology and to get certified in movement therapy. My dream is to finish school and to incorporate martial arts into a movement type system. I want to reach women who are from abused families . . . from battering situations . . . with poor self-esteem. I want to reach people who might not do the martial arts. I'd like to open a center where counseling is available along with the movement/martial arts."

Annie

If I had it to do over again . . . I wouldn't let my lover leave while I stayed home with my husband and children.

Annie is 50. She was born in England. She has bachelor's degrees in nursing and anthropology and a master's degree in philosophy. She is currently in transition and still married.

"I was married in 1963 and have been married 28 years. I am considering divorce now.

"It's been an O.K. marriage . . . nothing exceptional. We don't fight, we don't shout; I've never been abused. I'm getting out of it because I know I've been a lesbian for 16 years, and it's been very hard having to live a lie.

"I had a relationship with a woman for six and a half years. That was my first and only lesbian relationship. It broke up because she got a job out of state and I made a decision not to go with her. At the time my kids were teenagers, and I had to agonize over what to do. It was just an awful, awful decision. In the end, I decided that being a teenager was hard enough without my leaving. So, I made the decision to stay with them . . . to stay in the marriage for their sake. They are now 27 and 24, so I no longer have that same obligation to them.

"My husband knows. His response is, 'That's fine.' He is an engineer. My marriage was boring, but peaceful. After I told my husband, it's been pretty much the same as it's always been. We have been celibate for years. My husband suffers from clinical depression. Because of that, and the medications he has been on, his libido has diminished. Sex is not a big deal for him. He is emotionally tied to me and he doesn't want me to leave the marriage. He is happy for me to go and do what I have to do, but he doesn't want me to leave. I'm not sure if he has ever been in love with me. He is one of these people who never demonstrates any affection; he's never been very demonstrative.

"My lesbian relationship occurred when I was going to the university, back in the seventies. I got to know this woman who, I thought, was wonderful and I really enjoyed her. We were both political activists and she was out as a lesbian. At first it was nothing sexual. It was just a good friendship. I had known her for three years and then one afternoon something happened and I became incredibly sexually attracted to her. It was just an amazing feeling. I had never felt that for anyone before. We arranged to meet the following day and we ended up in bed. We spent most of the day in bed. It was wonderful! I discovered what sex was all about.

"We knew each other for six and a half years. All this time my husband didn't know. It sounds strange, but actually it was very easy not to let him know. I would cross the bridge and go to school and be with her, and then, in the evening, I would put on the other hat and cross over and be a mom. It was easy, but I was really two different people. It was easy because my life was so compartmentalized.

"I didn't seek counseling because I was too happy. My happiness outweighed any feelings of confusion I might have had. I was very busy with my relationship and school and just doing so many political things. I didn't have an awful lot of time to think about it. Then she got a job in Illinois and moved.

"I'm now at the stage where I'm trying to see how to go about this change . . . to see what steps to take to leave my marriage. My counselor's advice is to go very slowly and to be sure of every step.

"I'm out selectively at work; five or six people know. Most of those people are lesbians and are really good friends. I used to have a circle of lesbian friends, but I really cut myself off from the community when my lover left. So, in the past year I've been picking up the pieces a bit and making new contacts and new friendships. I've gone to the local lesbian center to an Over Forties group. I met a few people through that and I joined another lesbian group for professional women.

"I have a mother in England. I don't get on with her at all so I have no desire to tell her about my sexuality. I was abused by her as a child, verbally and emotionally. It was only about

10 years ago that I realized what had happened to me. I'm working through an awful lot of anger. I'll probably never see my mother again. The only reason I would tell her would be out of spite, and I don't want to use it like that. I feel too joyful, it shouldn't be something used in spite or rage.

"I am not out to my children yet. It's the next thing that I'll be doing. I haven't told them yet because I don't want to hurt them. I'm worried about what they'll think and how it will affect them. Having come from such a lousy childhood, I wanted to be to my kids everything that my mother was not to me. There will be a need to tell them because when I leave home they will want to know why I'm leaving. I've been in the closet so long I need to do this. It will be such a relief. I don't find it so difficult to maintain secrecy, except with the kids; that's difficult. I want to get over that hurdle.

"I don't think I have a lot of fun in my life at the moment. I am very busy. I'm just learning to live again. About a year ago, I became incredibly depressed. I couldn't sleep. I'd wake up at 2:00 every morning, no matter what. I couldn't eat; I had no appetite. I lost about 50 pounds. It was a really bad time, culminating in coming out to my husband.

"During that time, I couldn't do anything fun. I'm feeling well again and I'm just starting to do things for myself. My husband is so depressed that he doesn't want to do anything, ever. So, for so many years we haven't done anything. He just reads. I felt I was being dragged down into his depression. So now I've decided that I really have to look out for myself, and I have to make my own happiness outside of the marriage . . . outside of the home. I'm starting to get to know people and making plans to do things.

"At the age of 50, clearly, I have to think about the future. I don't earn very much myself financially, and it is going to be very, very hard. It's really scary. My degree in nursing is from London University and was so many years ago that it isn't of any worth now. I work as a medical assistant in a doctor's office. I am not licensed as a nurse in this country, since it would have been like starting all over again to try to get licensed.

"I have lived in the U.S. for 26 years. There is no market for my other degrees. I don't look forward to retirement. I am not currently seeing anyone. I don't have any special person I can go to or spend the rest of my life with. I just don't know about the future.

"If I had it to do over again, I wouldn't make the decision I made; I wouldn't let my lover leave while I stayed home with my husband and children. I regret it very much. I've seen her just three times since she left, and we talk once or twice a year on the phone. In the past couple of years, she has been in a relationship.

"I have a lesbian therapist, and that has been a godsend to me. It was real important to me that she be a lesbian. The last thing I wanted was to go to someone who would want to cure me. The organized lesbian groups have been very supportive. I've done a lot of reading on lesbian subjects, and now I don't have to hide these books.

"I regret so much getting married so young; I was 21. I knew I didn't love my husband, but it was back in the time when you looked at getting married as incredibly important. It was your meal ticket, and women needed to think about those things. I didn't think of it so consciously then, but I had very few options at the time. I thought nobody else would come along, and I had to find myself a man! I regret that hugely.

"I told my kids to use their twenties to grow up and enjoy life. They are both doing that. Neither of them is interested in settling down yet. I'm really pleased; I've done that right.

"I'm scared about the future. I wish I'd done this younger. Right now I'm thinking of getting out and being on my own, and being self-sufficient. I've never lived on my own—ever—so that's a big step for me.

"It's really scary; I don't know how I'm going to manage financially. I think I'll try to get into group living with some other women."

Lulu

It was a real sense of homecoming for me.

Lulu is 44. She was born in Montana. She has a B.A. degree in English literature and is taking courses at the university in hopes of getting into a master's program. She is an aspiring writer.

"I got married in 1966 and was married for 16 years until my husband was killed in an accident in 1982. When we married, I was 18 and my husband was 20 and we were very young for our ages. It wasn't the best marriage in the world, judging from others that I've seen. Yet, it wasn't the worst, either.

"The happiest part of the marriage was the first three or four years. There wasn't any kind of abuse or drinking or anything like that, but certainly a lot of ups and downs. I had two children, who both passed away. He was in the service, so there were periods of time that we were separated.

"After he left the service and for the better part of our marriage, he worked two jobs. I also worked, so, we didn't have a lot of time to spend together. After we had been married 11 years, we adopted two children—first a daughter, then a son. They are now 15 and 13, and they live with me.

"To decide that I was going to be a lesbian took years. I think when I was still married I had fantasies involving women. I never acted on them because it just didn't seem right. I was in Montana, and I didn't want to go to California, and I didn't want to wear leather boots!

"After my husband passed away, I tried to start dating men again. I really didn't want to because my good comfort levels were with women; getting together and talking and having a good time was always with women. I tried to date, and it was just awful. I was miserable and I made the man miserable. I was just not a nice person on these dates. I didn't think they were very nice either, but that might have had to do with where I was coming from.

"I gave up dating but still hadn't come to terms with my relationship with women. Then, slowly, I came to realize that it was possible to pursue this dream that seemed so outrageous to me. I had a phone number to call, and I must have called that number 50 times and hung up. Finally, I did call, and the gentleman gave me the number of a couple of women who were in a partnership. I called them and I got to know them better than a lot of my friends. They were very helpful and they invited me to go to the Metropolitan Community Church.

"I was terrified to do this, but I did it. It was a real sense of homecoming for me; it was wonderful! There were moments when I would have second thoughts, like the first time I went into a gay bar. It wasn't that it seemed wrong . . . it was just that it was something I had never seen before. These women I had talked with didn't paint a pretty picture. They said it was a very hard and difficult life, and that acceptance was hard to come by. They were very frank and honest; they talked about the good as well as the bad. This was in about 1984. My mindset has changed in an extraordinary fashion over these years.

"The first woman I started seeing was a woman a couple of years younger than I. I don't know whether you'd even call it a relationship because I just started having coffee with her and we went to a bar. It was very comfortable being with her. Then we moved on and started having romantic things. I didn't have any problem with it, but she had a problem with it because she didn't want to do anything unless there was a commitment, and I wasn't prepared to do that.

"I didn't storm the bars and start picking up women right and left. I don't do that; I never did. I've only been with four women. The second one was someone I was very attracted to; she was from California, and that was just a weekend thing. We still communicate. She is a lovely person and I enjoy her. The third person I was with for four years. We are not together anymore; we just found the differences were too great.

"I am currently in a year-old relationship; it is wonderful. It has its problems, but I think there is enough maturity and caring and sameness in our outlook that this one will work. I really hope it does because I really enjoy this woman's company.

"I consider myself a lesbian now. My children don't like that at all. My son's pretty O.K. with it, except when his friends come over for the night. He requests that we sleep in separate bedrooms. He is also uncomfortable with that—because it is a lie. He would rather have the lie, though, than us sleeping together. My daughter thinks it's just awful. Her dearest wish is that I find some rich, handsome man. When I first told her that I was a lesbian she said, 'No, you're not!' That's been about four years ago, and she still hasn't really accepted it.

"My partner has been in other relationships before, and the other women have always lived with her. This time, she is living with me; she's never done that before. That's one of the things that's causing an adjustment problem. In addition, two acting-out teenagers don't make life very easy, either. My children like her, but I have the impression that it wouldn't make any difference who it was or of what gender; there would always be some resentment. They want more of my attention.

"My kids are involved with a lot of sports activities. My previous partner went everywhere with me. We would go to my son's games, and everyone was really aloof and no one would talk to me. Then we would go to my daughter's sporting events and everyone was just wonderful. We came to be very good friends with several of those people. They were couples. We would go to parties and have them over for dinner. Nobody in that group has ever said anything, and it had to be obvious to them. That's kind of pleasant, and it doesn't bring you to the point where you have to blurt things out.

"I told my younger brother and sister quite some time ago, and as I told them, they just kind of sat there. Now they seem to feel O.K. with it. With the exception of me, my family doesn't talk much.

"My parents are living and my stepmother knows I'm a lesbian. I just told her last summer. When I talked with her, she said, 'Oh, I'm not surprised with all you've been through.' She didn't want me to tell my father, as she thinks it would kill him.

"I was prepared to tell him. We were sitting down at the dinner table and he jumped up and watched T.V. I just couldn't after that. So I just told her, and she was pretty horrified. They now live in Arizona, and I see very little of them. It is not something that I'm faced with frequently. Maintaining my secret isn't much of an issue for me.

"When I realized that being straight wasn't an option for me, I found that the hard part was being honest with the people I had been around for all those early years . . . husbands and wives and their kids whom I knew when I was married. That's still really uncomfortable for me. Some of these people are not very open-minded as far as any kind of change. In fact, they are bigots. It was hard and it is one of the reasons I decided to move.

"Widows and divorced women go through a different experience. It has to do with men wanting to be there for us, sometimes in a sexual way. They sometimes mean well, but they keep an eye on you, and you wonder about their motives.

"If a woman were contemplating changing her sexual orientation, the very first thing I would advise her to do would be to talk to somebody who is in the lifestyle . . . perhaps a therapist or a minister at the Metropolitan Church. I'd suggest going to places where there are lesbians and gay men and find out what your comfort level is. It might be a shock because it's not what we're used to.

"I would also suggest going to the bookstores and reading. Most towns of any size have bookstores who will order lesbian-oriented books."

Kristen ↙

*While I was married, I was totally unaware. I thought all
lesbians lived in San Francisco!*

Kristen is 39. She was born in Elk City, Oklahoma. She is in college
working toward a B.S. in nursing. She works as an LPN now at a
hospice for AIDS patients.

"I was married in 1970, and it lasted for 12 years. I dated an
older man when I was in high school and I married him the day
I graduated. I moved right out of my mother's house into his.

"It was a very chaotic marriage. I had a lot of emotional
problems and dealt with a lot of depression. He had problems,
too, but I don't think he dealt with them. There were a lot of
times when we really enjoyed each other's company, but
overall, it was very hard. We had a lot of arguing and a lot of
instability. It seems we took turns trying to leave each other
and the other one would be threatening suicide and be really
devastated.

"His goals were a lot different from mine. I enjoyed the
relationship, and home, and a lot of continuity. He wanted to
be a go-getter professionally and to make a lot of money. He
was a very hard worker; he worked over 80 hours a week, and
I felt abandoned. We fought about that a lot. He worked as a
financial analyst and on the side we owned a tavern. He was
either at one job or the other, and I got fed up with that. He
finally moved out of the home to do more things he wanted to
do. I finally just wanted the marriage over. We had one child.
She's 19 years old now.

"While I was married, I was totally unaware. I thought all
lesbians lived in San Francisco. Every so often, my husband
would rent pornographic movies and I would often watch
them with him. There often were scenes with two women, and
I would be aroused by that. I think I had had attractions toward
some women friends but I just dismissed them. I told my

husband that if I weren't married to him, I'd probably investigate those feelings, but it wasn't an option to me when I was married.

"I consider myself a lesbian now, but I wonder if I'm truly bi-sexual. I choose to be in a lesbian lifestyle, and I really enjoy it a lot. I am currently in a relationship which has continued for a little over five years. My lesbianism played no part in the breakup of my marriage.

"I guess what led me to explore my lesbianism was that there was a woman who was an obvious dyke at the place where I worked. She used to flirt with me, and I started flirting back, and we had a little fling. That kind of propelled me into investigating the gay lifestyle. I visited bookstores and did a lot of reading and talking to other people. I went to the Seattle Counseling Service and talked to a counselor there. I did a lot of thinking about it.

"After my exploration, I immediately got into a relationship! I've been a recovering alcoholic for seven years. While doing my exploration, I was becoming disillusioned because the people I met were also other alcoholics. I started feeling that that's just what we all were. Anyway, I met this woman at a bar, and we were very attracted to one another and we stayed together for three years. My getting clean and sober ended that. After that, I fell in love with another woman and we were together for about a year.

"Then, I met my current partner in 1985 at an AA meeting. This relationship is going great. A little over three years ago we had a commitment ceremony. We feel very married. We've bought a home together, and we are doing a lot of work on that home and it's very rewarding. We do go to couple's counseling to learn to live together better. It's been really helpful.

"My child lived with her dad after I left until her last year of high school, and then she came to live with us. She's out on her own now. Once I had made the decision that I was indeed a lesbian, I talked to her about it. She was about nine years old. I talked to her in terms of relationships. She was one of the first people I talked to about it. I felt it was important for her not to be confused about what she saw and heard. I wanted her to feel she knew what was going on.

"I think she was worried that she wouldn't have as much attention from me. I think it would have been the same if I had been dating men. Now she is very accepting. She went through a stage where, while accepting, she wanted to keep it very separate in her life. She didn't want other people to know. She was fearful of reactions from her friends. She is now very loving toward both my partner and myself and she is very supportive of our relationship. It feels great.

"I'm out to everybody. My mother, who has died, knew I was gay. She was worried about me being shunned by society. She didn't want me to tell my grandmother or my father because she was worried about their reactions. After my mother died, I told my grandmother and she has been my biggest supporter. She has been right there. We don't see much of my father, but he also is supportive. It feels good because he's made quite an effort to understand.

"I work at a facility now where the clientele are gay and most of the people who work there are gay. I have worked in more traditional institutions where I've been out, and for the most part I haven't had any overtly bad reactions. I did feel somewhat estranged from the straight people who talked about their families and didn't acknowledge my relationship.

"In the future, I hope to be in a steady job. I hope to be finished with school. I'd like to be doing hospice care. I hope to do some graduate work, maybe get a master's.

"I'd like to stay in the home we have. I feel really comfortable here."

out?

Jane

Aha! So that's it. There isn't anything wrong with me; I was just with the wrong sex!

Jane is 44. She was born in Providence, Rhode Island. She has a B.A. degree is psychology with minors in Hebrew and women's studies.

"I eloped when I was not quite 18, in 1965. I did not want to be around my mother, and that seemed to be the way out. I would have my own house and my own husband—and she couldn't tell me what to do.

"A few months after the elopement, we had a church wedding. The marriage lasted about two years, and then kind of back and forth for another couple of years and another kid. I have two children, both from that first marriage. The marriage ended because he had lots of affairs and I finally got fed up with it. My children now are 25 and 23.

"I married my second husband because he threatened to commit suicide if I didn't. I fell for it! He was scheduled to go for a one-year tour of duty in the Indian Ocean. We got married and he left the next week. He pulled his little schtick and I fell for it, and I married him. That was 1975 or 1976. I don't remember which. It lasted three years.

"I initiated the divorce for several reasons. He was a manic-depressive, but I didn't know it at the time I married him. The mood swings were really incredible. There were many, many explosions. During his manic phases, he was really nuts sexually. He would just be out doing his thing all over the place. He finally went into a hospital. Then he got out, and while celebrating New Year's Eve in a bar, he left me. I was dancing with friends, and I came back to the table and he was gone. He took my car. I had to borrow a dime to call him, and he said, 'You weren't coming home with me anyway.' I said, 'O.K., then I shan't.' That was the night Janet and I got together. She was my first lover.

"I had met Janet about a week before the bar episode. I had gone to a friend's house, and she came in. She was five feet, nine inches, 120 pounds of muscle and 21 years old! I was 34. That was a little over 10 years ago. We were together for four years, and she is still very dear to me. We talk on the phone all the time. She taught me a lot.

"When I look back on it, I see why I couldn't make those marriages work, even though one was dysfunctional. I always felt that something was wrong with me. It was just like, 'Nope, not that one. Nope, not that one.' I wondered how many men I was going to go through. I had very intense and intimate relationships with women, though not sexual. It never occurred to me to be sexual. It simply was not a part of my frame of reference.

"My second husband was the one who planted the seed in my mind. He did one of the typical male fantasies—'I want to see you with another woman.' When we would go out in public he would say, 'Oh, look at that one! Look at that one!' I finally told him that he was not going to pick out the woman I go to bed with; I'll pick her out. I'll find her somewhere.

"So, I did. I did that a couple of times. I finally said to him that my happiness was not going to lie with a man. I told him that I could feel that I was going to be with a woman. This was probably a year before we got divorced.

"Then I met Janet. She walked into the room, and people were all talking about going to The Bar that night. I didn't know what The Bar was. Somebody asked me if I was going to The Bar and I looked at her and asked if she was going to The Bar and she said, 'Yes.' And I said, 'Then I'm going to The Bar.'

"That relationship ended because we grew apart. She was growing up and had things to do, and I wasn't really ready to go back and do certain things over again. The age difference was too great and we just went our own ways.

"I am currently in a relationship. We're not wearing each other's rings, but we have been together for about a year and a half. I'm not in a position to live with her right now what with helping my children and my granddaughter and all. But my lover and I have fun together. Just living is fun.

"I never sought counseling. When I met Janet, I never went back home. That was it. It was like, 'Aha! So that's it! There isn't anything wrong with me; I was just with the wrong sex!' Now everything I can possibly do with women, I do. Men . . . you'd better give me your card because I'll never remember who you are.

"Some women have very nice marriages. They have a home and children and a standing in the community. I didn't leave anything like that. My children were with me all the time.

"I came out to my son. I took him for counseling and I went with him. He told the counselor that if his mom was happy, then so was he. He is now 23 and still sweet, but he is a Dead Head. He follows the Grateful Dead around. He winters at my house. He comes in with nothing but the rags on his back, and we rerobe him and he sleeps and he takes baths and eats lots of food. He gets to go to the dentist and gets physical care, and then the weather warms up and he leaves. He panhandles and works on the sanitation crew of the Grateful Dead. What a way to live! I don't know how long this will go on.

"My relationship with my daughter is fine now. Her problems started before I came out. I finally know what caused that sweet little 12-year-old to turn into a banshee: it was sexual abuse by my second husband. I didn't know that at the time. It was a textbook case. He told her, 'Don't say anything to your mother because she won't believe you; she'll believe me. She'll throw you out because she loves me.' She didn't tell me, but she acted out. It's a wonder one of us didn't kill the other one over that couple of years before she finally just took off.

"She is now making progress, but she is very negative and has low self-esteem. She has an over-eating problem. We are taking it one step at a time. She lives with me and has a two-year-old daughter. She actually said, about a week ago, that she was going to check out the counseling center and see what they have available. All those decisions have to come from her, not from me. She is going to the university, and doing well. This is a kid with a genius I.Q. She was invited to join MENSA when she was eleven. My children are not closeted about me. My daughter used to use my lesbianism as a weapon, but she doesn't now.

"I can't think of anybody I'm not out with. I'm out at work, and it is fine. Right now, I sell copiers because it pays the bills. Earlier, I worked for a company as a customer care rep, which was mostly instructing. I loved that job. Then about a year and a half ago, the company eliminated my position for financial reasons, so I went on unemployment and looked and looked for a job. Finally, after eight months of unemployment, the sales manager called up and asked me if I would like to sell copiers. I said to myself, 'No, but I need a job,' so I took it.

"My mother knows I'm lesbian. I don't know if my father does. My mother lives in California with her fifth husband. My father, to the best of my knowledge, is still living in Atlanta. My mother's reaction was, 'Oh my God, we don't discuss that.' She refuses to acknowledge her great-granddaughter because she does not approve of the circumstances of her birth: my daughter did not marry the father. This is from a woman who, before she divorced my father, ran away and had two children by other men! She had a very convoluted series of marriages and affairs. My grandmother raised me. One time, my half brothers and sisters had to be taken away and put in foster homes. So here is this woman not acknowledging my grandchild. I am not speaking to her right now.

"In the future, I see myself being secure and settled in a job with a retirement plan. I need to be tracking and working toward that 65th year. I do not want to be a bag lady! I hate selling copiers!

"My dream would be that I would get a Ph.D., and that I would be teaching women's studies courses at the university. I'd love a house out in the woods, and I would write. These are my dreams."

Ann

*When I first had a relationship with a woman, it seemed
easy and simple, and very sweet and clear.*

Ann is 35. She is currently in her third year of a four-year college
degree and is studying math. She plans to go into computer science.
She is working as an inventory planner, having worked her way up
in the company over the last 11 years.

"I was married in 1976. We lived together three years but
were legally married five. He was a nice man. He has since
remarried and has two children. We haven't kept in contact.

"We met in sixth grade, started going steady at the beginning of high school, and we were engaged when we graduated.
He went away to college and we were married a year and a half
later and lived 1,400 miles from home. The marriage was very
hard because we were both very young and were at an age
where we were changing a lot.

"We started off with me working and him in school. We
finally decided that we would each work part-time and both go
to school. There were government grants available and we
took advantage of them. Being full-time students and working
was a rough schedule to keep. We had no children, which was
one of our biggest issues. He wanted children and I didn't. So,
after three years we separated.

"During our separation, I was taking women's studies in
college and found myself in a wonderful group of women. One
by one, they came out to me—and I was suddenly surrounded
by a group of lesbians. I liked them.

"I was twenty-three when I first had a relationship with a
woman. My thought, then, was that I had choices that other
people didn't have. I considered myself bi-sexual. I think
sexually I would still claim that label, but emotionally I am
definitely over into the lesbian side. Emotionally . . . that's the
big one.

"My first relationship was with a close friend. As a matter of fact, my ex-husband introduced us. It lasted for as long as I was in town, and she and I are still in touch.

"We were more friends than lovers. We never considered ourselves partners; we were very definitely loving friends. It ended because I left town.

"There were subsequent relationships with women, and I backslid once. I decided at one point that women only broke my heart and they were nothing but trouble. I was having no more of them so I started hanging out with a man friend of mine and one thing led to another. He and I went out for two years and talked about getting married. I talked of our living together but when it came time to give notice at my apartment, I couldn't do it. Besides, I was cheating on him with a woman. I'm not proud of that but it did let me know where my loyalties really were.

"I am currently in a relationship. It will be five years in March, and it is wonderful. We have a house together and two wonderful dogs. The two of us have decided we don't want children.

"I'm out with my mother but I didn't tell my stepfather. He's been over to the house, and he knows. He's never said anything. I'm not in contact with my father.

"My mother won't discuss it; it's a little strange. This Christmas the two of them invited my partner and me out for dinner. They insisted I bring her along, and they had a gift for her. I'm surprised sometimes at how well they take it. Then there are other times when Mother has made it pretty clear that she is not happy about this.

"I have no brothers or sisters. My mother told me she wanted grandchildren, and I told her to go ahead and have them, that I had no objection! That probably wasn't the right thing to say but that's what rolled off my tongue.

"My partner is out with her family. For years, her father has been a deacon in the Baptist church. This is pretty touchy. They are not happy about the situation either. She came out when she was 16 and they went through all the trauma associated with that before I ever came along. By the time she met me, they thought I was just another one. Then, when we bought the house and it really seemed like this was going to be pretty stable, they have come around in a big way.

"They invite us both to go to stay with them. Her mother and I exchange letters, and she got me started growing African violets, which I love. Now I've got her started on orchids. They put us in the same room at their house in a double bed. She says that her parents like me better than they like her because I'm closer to the daughter they always wanted.

"I am not out at work. That would be a no-no. I'm out to some straight friends and actually a few people at work, but not very many. I'm pretty careful about who I come out to. I make pretty sure it's going to be positive before I open my mouth. For the people I don't want to know, I say *my* house and *my* dogs. I'm used to being on my toes about the lesbianism. At first it was very difficult. Working where I work in a stuffy corporate environment, you can't be your at-home relaxed self anyway. I just think of it as part and parcel of the job.

"My advice for women who are thinking of being with other women is to be gentle with yourself. You don't have to make all of your life decisions at once. Understand that it's a process. I think somebody told me that at the time and I had no idea what they were talking about. Just take it slow and easy. It's not an easy thing to go through. It may be the best road for you, but that isn't always the path of the least resistance.

"I do think that having been married is more common than we usually talk about. I think there are a lot more of us around than most people would think.

"If you want to meet other lesbians, I don't really know where you find them. If I were single right now, I don't know what I'd do. I don't like bars and I don't play softball. Finding the community is difficult. I, too, was afraid of dykey women but now it seems to me the more leather they wear the more like teddy bears they are.

"When I first had a relationship with a woman, it seemed easy and simple, and very sweet and clear. It didn't seem like a thorny issue to me. It felt like 'This is wonderful.' The problems I came up against both from the outside and the inside happened quite a bit later and over a long period of time.

"It doesn't take too long to develop the attitude that if other people don't like it, they don't have to; that's up to them. But, for yourself to like it takes more work and it crops up in ways that can be really unexpected . . . like being seen together in public by somebody from high school. There are things you didn't foresee at all.

"The company had a party for their 10-year people recently, and I went alone. I knew I could bring a 'date' as I know a lot of men from one of the AIDS support groups. I could have asked a friend to come with me, but I decided not to do that. I didn't need to hide behind it.

"Being a lesbian was easy at first, and I thought it was going to continue that way. It's been 12 years now, and things still crop up.

"I don't think it's possible to grow up in this society without being homophobic, and I was. I was scared of lesbians who looked tough. I used to have a terrible time in my own community.

"I don't go to bars much anymore, but when I did, they would look at me like I was lost. This happened one night after I'd been to a play. It was a Friday night and I didn't want to just go home. I had been in the straight world for a week. I was single at the time so I needed to be around my own kind.

"There I was in my dress and heels and my hair piled up on my head, and with all the war-paint. I'd been first at work and then out to the theater. I walked into a women's bar . . . just stopped off on my way home for a drink. You should have felt the tension in the place!

"I walked in the door and everybody sort of panicked. Here I thought, 'I came to be comfortable and look what I'm getting.' I sat there with my drink and sort of smiled and thought to myself, 'Let them be uncomfortable. It's their problem.'

"Then, to my surprise, a friend of mine who was playing pool in the back saw me and said, 'Hey!' and there was this collective sigh of relief. The phobia can work both ways."

Mary

I'd like to take a poll of my straight women friends to see if they have ever been attracted to women, just to see if I am really very different from them.

Mary is 40. She was born in Kansas. She has a master's degree in education and works at a software company.

"I was married in 1972, when I was in college working on my bachelor's degree. I was only 20 and it was my declaration of independence from my parents. But, I just kind of transferred my dependence to him. It was pretty much a disaster from beginning to end.

"We were married for a total of four years, two of which I was still in college. Then, I had a teaching job, and it seemed very odd to be acting like a professional during the day and then go home and be treated like a child. So, I initiated the divorce. That was one of the biggest steps that I had ever taken on my own behalf. I was single for four years before I remarried.

"I went into the service and I met Fred. We did a lot of traveling together and were very good friends. I had a lot of respect for him and I had fun with him. We were married when I was 28. When he finished his tour of duty, he started going to school at a community college, and I found out I was pregnant with Terri. I separated from the military a month before I had Terri, and a year later we moved. He finished his undergrad degree at the university, and things were really rough financially.

"Fred got management jobs in restaurants, and I was at a publishing job, but we weren't earning very much money. We tried to make sure that Terri's needs were met and that we were able to spent lots of time with her. We were really, really stressed.

120

"I have a lot of grief over the whole breakup. We had a big commitment, and it's hard to watch those dreams just disintegrate. We were together for 10 years and have been separated now for two. He lives a couple of blocks from Terri and me. This is intentional so that we can share parenting.

"The marriage broke up, but we're not divorced yet. I'm the one who left. I think it wasn't one person's fault. There were some things that combined to make things rough for us. We felt very isolated from family support, had odd work schedules and a lot of financial pressures. The two of us made a lot of intentional sacrifices. We put our child ahead of our relationship. For me there was a lack of spiritual sharing; we basically quit growing. I felt like I was just cheerleading this thing on. We just looked at things so completely differently.

"Somewhere along the line, I just decided to stop the cheerleading, and the marriage just crumbled. I think he had been wanting this to happen but wasn't going to initiate it. I don't place all the blame on him because he was busy trying to make a living. He had no emotional energy left over for his home life.

"He had an affair when Terri was in kindergarten. I was outraged. I felt we had been off to such a good start, and we were such good friends, and how could somebody violate that trust? All that did was to expose the fact that we had big problems.

"One of these problems was that I became very disinterested in sex. I still can't decide whether that had to do with a lack of emotional sharing; I think so many women feel that way about men. I don't know how much of that was tied up with my now discovered lesbianism; I have no way of knowing.

"That whole year that Terri was in kindergarten, there were a lot of painful things going on. We never fought in front of her; in fact, we hardly fought. We just had a more icy silence. Just nothing going on. I started sleeping out on the couch instead of in the bed. That went on for a very long time. He didn't like it, but we just weren't connecting.

"It took me a long time to get to the point where I would admit that the marriage was going to break up. I knew I wanted to leave and live by myself again. I was remembering those years when I did live by myself and fantasizing about having my own apartment and leading my own life again. But, I felt like I had this weight on my shoulders. I wondered how I could afford to live alone.

"Anyway, I started seeing a counselor. She told me that if a woman decides to leave a marriage she can usually find a way to make it happen. I kept that in my mind. I had decided that once I was done with my marriage and out of there that I was done with men. I decided that wasn't any good because, emotionally, there is just nothing there. It would have to be a very special person; I didn't want to have anything more to do with a relationship for a long time. I thought I would concentrate on my friendships with women, and my activities, and be celibate if that's what it meant. I just wanted to live life fully. I didn't need to have men anymore.

"So, I was still married, but that's where I was emotionally. One day Ellen came into this publishing company to work. I ended up working very closely with her, and we immediately became friends. A couple of weeks after she started work, she was talking about a relationship she had just gotten out of and she used the word 'she.' She told me that I knew something about her that she didn't always talk about to people. She seemed to want to check my reactions and make sure I was O.K. with it. That was fine with me.

"I had known gay men in the past, but really the only lesbian I had known was someone who wouldn't have interested me anyway. Ellen would talk and I asked her lots of questions about lesbianism. She was ready to tell me her perspective on things. She had been a lesbian ever since her adolescent years. She came out at 19 in college—and never looked back.

"We had long conversations about sexuality. I said that if all the cultural things were left out of it, we'd all be bi-sexual. She said that for her part that wasn't so. She said that on a continuum she'd be on the queer side. Finally she asked me if I had ever been attracted to a woman and I told her that I had been.

"I have been attracted to women all along. It was just taboo that women don't talk about those things. I'd like to take a poll of my straight women friends to see if they have ever been attracted to women, just to see if I am really very different from them. I just don't know. If the marriage had not crumbled, I don't know whether I would have explored any of this.

"So . . . Ellen invited me to a movie that she had known I wanted to see. It was a really powerful, spiritually oriented movie. I said that Fred would probably like to come, too—even though I wasn't wild to have him come. I just thought he should come, too. We were sitting there in this movie and I was just a basket case. I was moved to tears with all the things that were going on. Ellen was on my right and Fred was sitting on my left, giving me no feedback at all. I'm sure he was thinking, 'There she goes again doing her usual blubbering.'

"I was deeply moved inside, and all I wanted to do was throw my arms around Ellen and sob. All of a sudden, it just came to me with this great clarity that one could have that really close connection with another woman. All of a sudden it wasn't theory anymore. I understood how that could be.

"I didn't say anything about that to Ellen. As things went on in our friendship, it just became evident that she was interested in me, but cautious because of the fact that I was married. She also knew the status of that marriage. I started keying into her and her body and thinking what it would be like to be with a woman. Things just started developing from there.

"So, now I am with her. We have been together two years. This is not what I would have planned. I would have planned that I would be a single person and gotten over all those other wounds first. I wasn't planning to look for a relationship. I hadn't considered women yet. I was just going to be myself. But that's not how it happened. It is wonderful! She is the only woman I've ever had as a lover. I feel this is going to be a very stable relationship.

"My husband knows I'm a lesbian now. I don't know that he has a response to the lesbianism. He is very hurt that I'm in a relationship, and now he'd like to make our marriage work.

What's interesting is that a co-worker where he works who has been helpful to him happens to be lesbian. I've never met her but my daughter really likes her.

"That was how Fred found out about Ellen. My daughter would talk about all the time she was spending with us, and I would not try to make her edit her conversation. She needed to be able to talk about whatever she wanted to. So I figured that sooner or later he was going to want to know. He did want to know, and I had to tell him.

"My daughter is 10 now and she knows I'm a lesbian. That has been ongoing, too. She had participated with me in freedom rallies before any of this happened. I believe that one deliberately teaches children that the whole idea of being gay is not something to be shunned, or ashamed of, or spat on. I didn't want her to buy into any prejudices. I explained in sequential stages about Ellen and about our relationship. She finally asked me several months ago if I were a lesbian. I answered by saying I wasn't sure; that things can change. I told her I wasn't quite sure what I would call myself. Since then I had another talk with her and I told her that if a woman loves another woman, and if that's the way things seem to be, that the name for that is 'lesbian.' I told her that was what I was.

"I don't think the subject has come up at her school. I think as far as peer pressure goes, she would think twice before she would let them know that her mom is a lesbian. Even though she is young... kids, they are right there. They follow this stuff. At our church her friends know that I'm with Ellen, and that is fine.

"I have not talked to my mother about being a lesbian. I'm just going to have to wait and see how it goes. She's pretty homophobic. Since I don't live close to her, I'll just see.

"I try to be discreet. I'm only now beginning to deal with the legalities of the divorce. It's just been too much to think about emotionally. I am acutely aware of the fact that I have legal binds to this other person. I could jeopardize the custody of my daughter if I got too far out. Once I am divorced, maybe my closetedness will change.

"Five years from now I hope I will be with this woman. I don't think I'm going to need experiences with different women. We listen to a lot of music. We go to a lot of movies. We read a lot of books. We both like to do outdoorsy types of things. Spiritually, we are in sync and getting more so all the time. We like our sex.

"One part of me is glad I had the marriage and the child, and another part of me goes, 'Why didn't I know there were women out there?' I really celebrate this part of myself. I'm so glad to know about it."

Diane

*Once you've been a lesbian, why would you want to be
anything else? I find women much more exciting than men.
I find the sex so much more fulfilling.*

Diane is 63. She was born in New York City. She is a computer
programmer.

"I got married the first time for the simple reason that I had
no idea I had any choice. I was 20 and it was in 1948. It was
something that everyone did.

"Then, in 1953 while I was working as a key puncher, I
worked with this woman. I enjoyed her company very much.
I became very interested in her, but I had no idea of what was
going on. Looking back on it she was what could be considered
very obvious. She was very butch looking. She wore very
tailored suits.

"I knew about lesbianism but it never occurred to me that
I could be, or that anybody I knew could be. She finally told me
she was gay, and since I didn't know what that was, she told
me. I knew a woman lived with her. When she told me all that,
it made it O.K. for me to be interested in her. Up until then we
had just gone out for coffee and the like. Now, I wanted to go
out with her and I wanted her to take me to a gay place. So, we
went to a gay bar in the village. I invited her up to my
apartment while my husband was at work—and I had a
holiday.

"I had had some really strange ideas about what women
did together. I knew very little about sex and I disliked it
intensely with my husband. I had had one orgasm in my life.
Everything was, very bluntly, penis-oriented. My husband
didn't do any fancy stuff or anything. Certainly not any oral sex
. . . though I had read about women doing that and that
intrigued me.

126

"Anyway, Denise came over and I answered the door in a red nightgown. She kissed me and I had this crazy idea that women wore dildos and I thought she had forgotten to put it on. I thought that we wouldn't be able to do anything!

"In spite of the fact that I hated sex, I was looking forward to doing something. We kissed and she made love to me and I wasn't able to do anything. She thought she hadn't made me happy but I said, 'No, I'm able to learn.' I wanted to do whatever it would take.

"A week later Denise and I found an apartment. I told my husband that I was leaving the next day. That was in 1953. We moved in together and we visited the gay places and I just loved it. I thought it was the most exciting thing. I liked being with her and I never never regretted what I did. It was easy for me. I never considered going for therapy. There weren't any books; there weren't any support groups. Only movie stars or people who were really messed up went to shrinks. This you had to do all by yourself.

"I thought about the fact that we would never have children. The second thought was what if she dies and I get left all alone. With my husband, I could never buy what I really wanted to buy. Everything we bought had to be because it was on sale or something that he wanted. He was such a penny pincher that I never had what I wanted. So with Denise I thought, 'Here are two women and we won't have that either.' Our tastes were so alike—we thought alike—she was fantastic.

"So, we lived together. One of her little things was that she was involved with another woman. Straight women just loved her. These women just came on to her and the fact I was with her didn't bother them at all. Just like it didn't bother me to go after her when she was with somebody. Eventually we got over all that and we lived together for eight and a half years. She was bright and funny and I just loved being with her. I never got tired of being with her.

"She had her little things on the side. Women would get interested in her and she would encourage them. There were times when I thought I couldn't handle it. Then, when push came to shove, she would say, 'O.K., I won't see her anymore.'

She would encourage me to get involved with somebody else, and I actually had a one night stand with a friend of ours who had always been after me. It didn't turn out to be much. I would have never left Denise.

"Unfortunately, after about a year together she started to show signs of something and we didn't know what it was. Every year she would have an attack and be sicker. She died of lupus erathematosis at the age of 31 in 1961. It was really very tragic. Even when she died, there wasn't anybody I could talk to. There weren't any support groups or anything.

"It took me years to understand about being gay. Denise was very butch and I had to be very femme. That was a no-touch situation, since it was the typical polarized relationship. Of course, women like that always say that women who are not like that don't know who they are. I thought I was femme. It was not as fulfilling as it might have been. She had me brainwashed, thinking this was the way I was. I loved her or I wouldn't have been with her for eight years, but I really didn't want to be with another heavy duty butch again. And, I couldn't see myself with another woman like myself. That left me very confused. I didn't understand and I had nobody to tell me anything different, so I didn't do anything for a long time.

"So, after a few years, I dated men and had a couple of affairs. I went to Puerto Rico for a few weekends to see where Denise came from, and then I moved there in 1963. I stayed down there and I dated men, and didn't think anything about gay life. But, when I was making love, I thought about women.

"Eventually, I met this man who was a lot younger than I was. We got married. I told him I had been gay, and it was O.K. with him. He was young and lonely. We married and had a child and everything was pretty good for a while. Then, we went on a trip to the Middle-East and he got it into his head that he really wanted to be with an Oriental girl. He liked anything that was different and liked to prove himself. I was pregnant with my second son at that point.

"When we got home, he said he didn't want to be married to me anymore and I said, 'That's great because I'm pregnant.' So he stayed with me. I really didn't want him to leave me because I was in my late forties and here I was with two kids. So we had this arrangement that I would be the wife and he would take me out occasionally, and we would make love every four days.

"I thought maybe he would be happy for awhile. But, eventually, he wanted to leave again. I didn't want to stay in Puerto Rico under those circumstances, so we moved to Texas. In '76 he decided he didn't want to be married to me any longer. He just went off one day to the Dominican Republic and got a divorce.

"I guess if he had wanted to stay married, I probably would have. I still didn't know that I had a choice. I'm not a dumb person; it has to do with how I was brought up. I felt being gay was something other people could have, but it wouldn't be for me. It just never occurred to me that I could lead a gay life.

"After the divorce he stayed around. He kept wearing his wedding ring and he still slept with me. We bought a house together. We went to Europe together. Nobody knew that we were divorced. He was always telling me not to count on his being around. The sex got harder for me. I thought that was because I was getting old and dried up and things like that. I would have plugged along anyway because I thought nobody would want me at my age and with two kids.

"I was kind of lonely and I met some guy at work. He was a programmer also, and we got involved. When my 'husband' came back from a trip, I told him that I had found somebody else. I went with this man for two and a half years until 1981. It was the last man I went with. He was 20 years younger than I was. It got rocky at the end because he wasn't as sophisticated and was much too young. After that, I went for a number of years with no sex.

"Then, one year, I went to Club Med and took my kids. I met this woman and we smoked some pot together, and she was so sexy and I seduced her. I thought that was terrific. I was the initiator and the aggressor. I was wondering in the back of my head if I would like it sexually. I had not been with a woman for 20 years.

"Finally, I went to therapy and my therapist said that I might be happier with women. I had had it in my head that this was because I couldn't get a man. It took me a few years after that. I had to leave it alone.

"Then I asked my veterinarian and her lover to take me to a gay bar. I was fascinated with it. I couldn't stay away and I made excuses to go in there. My kids were still young and they were a good excuse for not going out much on weekends.

"I finally got myself involved in a conversational group that met on Sunday mornings in '86, and then, I started doing more things. I started going to dances and to the bar on Saturday nights. In a few months, a woman I met really came on to me and asked me out. I knew this would be my opportunity. I was dying to know if this was what I really wanted. It turned out I liked the sex a lot with a woman, but I didn't care for her.

"I have been in my current relationship eight months. That is not a long time but that is the longest I've been with anybody in years. I enjoy being with her and she loves me very much. I have more things in common with her than I've had with anybody. But, we look at things very differently and I don't have the rapport I'd like to have with her. It bothers me sometimes but I'm trying to not worry about it because we have so many other good things together. As I get older, the sex gets better. I don't have to think of anything else and I can just enjoy it.

"My children are 16 and 18 and they are aware that I'm lesbian. In early '86 when I started to go to the discussion group at a church, I would leave them downstairs in a place for kids. They would stay there until time for lunch, and then I'd take them to lunch with these heavy duty lesbians. I told them about the lesbian dances and I told them what gay was. Then, I told them that I was gay also. They had played with the other lesbians' children. I asked them if they had any questions and one of them said, 'Yes, can we go to bed now?'

"I have asked them since how they felt about it. They said that they'd rather I weren't gay, but that's the way things are. They lived with me up until two years ago. The younger one

130

lives with his father and comes down here once a month. The older lives with another boy. He still doesn't listen to authority. We are all on good terms.

"I am not out at work. I have one buddy there who is 30, and he knows and likes it. He knows my partner. I'm not that friendly with anyone one else there. I marched in the gay parade last year and I'll do it this year. I don't care if I get on television. I don't think the straight people give two hoots.

"Once you've been a lesbian, why would you want to be anything else? I find women much more exciting than men. I find the sex so much more fulfilling.

"I'd tell women who are interested in other women to go for it. Talk with other people and get some advice. Read things. If you are attracted to women, you can be sure that that's where you ought to be. If you have an interest in the same sex, that's never going to leave you. You can become a nun or get married but you'll always think about it. I see nothing negative about being gay. I love being a lesbian."

Gayle

It wasn't so much women. . . . It was this particular woman!

Gayle is 38. She was born in the state of Washington. Gayle has a B.S. degree in nursing and works as a staff nurse.

"I was married in 1978; it lasted for seven years, although we were separated for the last two. I met Mack as I was finishing college and he was finishing up the last two years of his Ph.D. in electrical engineering. We were very good friends and we had a lot of things we wanted to do together. We both had a lot of fun, and for the beginning years of our marriage we were very compatible. We argued a lot, but we were never mean to each other. There was a lot of respect. I think it was a nice marriage for what I knew and needed then. But as all things go, my life got complicated.

"I fell in love with Sue, who shared an office with me at work, shortly after I was married. Both of us denied that it was anything more than a friendship, and neither of us wanted it to be anything more than a friendship. But in our heart of hearts, we knew. That went on for years. I would call it more sensuality than sexuality. It wasn't very sexual; it was mostly an affair of the heart. I just felt that I had finally fallen in love. As much as I loved Mack, I really questioned whether I'd ever fallen in love with him. It just was not the same. I never felt that I'd really *fallen* in love with the guy. That really tore me up.

"Finally, I realized that I needed to make a change. It was obvious that I was not in the right place. But I loved my house and I loved my neighborhood. I had wonderful friends within walking distance all around me. A bunch of us had all bought old farm houses at the same time and we were all fixing them up. There was a great sense of community.

"Even so, I knew that I was living a lie. It wasn't so much women. . . . It was this particular woman! Maybe that made it

132

easier for me. I didn't want to be a lesbian; I knew that much. I would have just as soon have been heterosexual. Now I have matured!

"At the time, I really wanted to be this good girl. I'd graduated from a good university; I'd married a very successful man. Maybe down the road we'd have some lovely children. I bought into that whole fairy tale, but it was unravelling. It was a mess, and I really wanted to pursue this relationship with Sue. So, I separated from him.

"I know now that my relationship with Sue was pretty classically dysfunctional and co-dependent. There was push-pull game-playing going on. Her control was around sex—I was very willing to be sexual and she was not. I was so in love with her that I didn't care. But as soon as I got out of my marriage, the relationship with Sue didn't work. She backed off and didn't want to have anything to do with it.

"So . . . live and learn. To this day, she hasn't done many long-term relationships. I don't know that she has ever lived with anyone in a committed relationship. She does not consider herself a lesbian. The last time I talked to her, she said she was 'omnisexual.' She doesn't like labels. We went through a period of time when we didn't see each other—because it just became so really horrible. Then, about two years ago, we happened to run into each other and got together again and tried to work on the friendship and that just didn't work either.

"When I first realized I was interested in women, I went to see a counselor and I couldn't tell the truth about it. I was so torn. I had this life that sort of worked, and I just didn't want to throw it all away. A part of me knew I had to. It would have been good if Sue had said she wanted to be with me, or made any clear messages about it. She told me flat out that she wasn't gay. I was just really confused; it was awful.

I didn't really see myself as lesbian; I thought I could go on either side of the fence. I'm one of these people for whom sexuality is kind of an option. I felt I had crushes on both men and women. Now, I think it would be hard to be with a man again. I don't rule it out. I have wonderful friendships with men, but I'm just not driven to be with men. My former husband wasn't a bad fellow. He did not mistreat me. He was my biggest fan. He was wonderful. He was kind.

"I have been in my present relationship six years. I'm really happy. Our hardest time was when I tried to re-establish that friendship with Sue. Actually, I ended up feeling like I was falling back in love with her. I don't regret doing it because, for me, it finalized things. It certainly was the hardest challenge that Jo and I will ever have, and because we were able to deal with it together, it took our relationship to a deeper level.

"I met Jo as a part of a basketball team. Then, some mutual friends of ours had a party and we got together. It was pretty obvious that there was a lot of attraction between us. She was partnered with a woman at the time, but that relationship had been falling apart for while. She had tried to make it work, but it was really over. I was the vehicle for making it really over. Once I met her, I just put everything else aside. I had had this short term relationship with a nineteen-year-old who was a wonderful person. But, as soon as I met Jo, I just tidied up things. I broke with the woman and finalized my divorce.

"I'm not out at work, except to certain people. I struggle a lot about coming out there. I think, 'Who are you going to come out to—the whole hospital?' Since I move around all over the hospital, I just made my own little rules. If I decide that I'm going to see any of the people I work with outside of work, I come out to them. I figure if they are on the planet and I talk about my partner, then they either get it or they don't. I don't have a lot invested in most of the people I work with. I don't want to know about their personal lives so why should I spill my beans!

"My ex-husband knows. We actually spent part of my last vacation together with mutual friends on their boat. I think for him it is an easy way to explain why he and I are not together. He never seemed to have any problem with it. I never got any sense that he thought it was disgusting or anything negative. He is really great.

"I come from a family of five. I'm a twin and we're the youngest. My twin sister and I are very close, and we live very different lifestyles. She is very comfortable with my lifestyle, and she likes my partner. She told me she has had a few brief affairs with women and she understands the attraction to women. It makes sense to her when she thinks of me. She is an alcoholic and she has a relationship with a man that is sort of on-again, off-again. She lived with one guy who was put in jail twice for beating her up. We've had more separation in the past 10 years then before, and I feel it's because of who she has been with and her chaotic lifestyle. Even though I'm gay, I feel I live a very conservative lifestyle compared to her. I've been in the same job for five years. I come home at night. I own my own home. I'm very typical. I don't think my being with women has been a problem at all.

"I have not come out to either of my brothers. My brother who lives in Georgia converted to Mormanism in his early twenties. He graduated from Brigham Young in police science, and he is very red necked. I don't see too much of him. I wouldn't be surprised if he knows. I have damn near said that I'm gay to my brother in San Diego. I think he knows, but he sometimes likes to think it's not real.

"I came out to my other sister. I knew she had a hard time with it, but I really feel that she has come around. My mother knew, as mothers know, as soon as Jo moved in with me. Now she openly talks about my being gay. She talks to her pastor about it. She includes Jo's name on cards.

"I bring my partner to every holiday family gathering. They are a lot less prejudiced than they used to be. I come from a family where four out of five children are divorced, and my mom is happy to see one of her kids settled. As for my father . . . I have never discussed it with him, and I don't know if my mother has. I think he knows. He would have to be an idiot, which he is not. I don't feel like I'm living much of a secret life.

"I am enjoying my life. For fun, I like to go boating, scuba diving and walking the beach. In summers, we go up north for skiing, hiking and backpacking. I like the out of doors. My dream is to build a house—all by myself—on the 10 acres of land that we own."

Claudia

To me, it was an adventure. It was like
coming home. . . . It fit.

Claudia is 46. She was born in New York City. She has had some
college and has worked in marketing.

"Both of my marriages were to the same childhood friend.
It was just assumed we would get married. We were married
about 35 days! I was 19, and I got pregnant. I was stupid, and
he trapped me.

"He was thrilled to death, but I hated being married. He
was a wonderful, sweet, and sensitive man. I hated sleeping
next to him! Sex was great, but the emotional part wasn't. I was
a kid . . . immature, stupid. He was in the Marines, stationed on
Whidbey Island, Washington. I was never there if I could help
it. He felt real bad about it not working out, and yet, I was done.
He dropped me off at my Dad's house and the look on my
Dad's face. . . 'What the hell are you doing here, 35 days later?'

"My husband and I tried to talk about it, but things got out
of hand, and I ended up getting a restraining order against him
just so he wouldn't be around me.

"After the baby was born, Dwayne came around again,
and then we started to talk. This was 1969. I had gone to see a
movie called *The Fox*, and it was like a light bulb had gone off
in my head. Things started to make sense. I didn't feel that
alienation I felt before. Meanwhile, Dwayne and I had been
talking and we had started dating again. I mentioned that film
to him, and he said, 'Oh, if you ever let a lesbian get hold of you,
you'll never go back to men.' It was weird. I said, 'Really?'

"Then, before we remarried, I had my first experience with
a woman. That put me into a total state of confusion! We went
out one night with his boss and his boss's wife. There was this
immediate attraction between her and me. I was blown away
at that point. She was older and sophisticated. We went back

to their house and the guys were out in the living room drinking and talking. We went back in her bedroom so she could change clothes and she kind of came on to me. She said, 'Dwayne is so crazy about you, you guys should be together. Why don't you get married again and we can carry on and nobody will ever know?'

"So, that night I told him that maybe we should get married again. We drove down to Reno that night. I thought it would be perfect. You talk about living in a dream world!

"He had no inkling—no idea. The minute I said, 'I do,' I said, 'What the hell did I do?' We tried to work it out, and that lasted about 40 days. I just couldn't deal with it. It was like being a teenager all over again. I was never home, and I finally told him about women. He said that that was O.K. with him because he loved me. He said, 'It's O.K. as long as you come home.'

"I still didn't feel right about it, and one night I didn't come home 'til about six in the morning. When I got home, my mom was there with him. He was close to my mom, and he had gone over in the middle of the night all upset and crying and told them everything. They both looked at me and—well, I will love him to this day. He just put his arms around me and said, 'I just want you to be happy. If that will make you happy—that's O.K.'

"That was my first understanding of unconditional love. The same with my Mom. She just asked me to see a psychiatrist to be sure that I was O.K., which I did, and he said I was fine. That's what happened. The boss's wife and I never really got together again. We saw each other for lunch a few times, but we had different schedules. I also sensed that she was an alcoholic and self-destructive; otherwise, I probably would have pursued it. But the world had opened up for me. I discovered women!

"My first woman lover was Olivia. This was in 1969, after Dwayne and I had broken up again. I was working for a figure-reducing salon, which was quite popular then. It was run by women. Those were crazy times. Anyway, there was an immediate attraction between Olivia and me. She certainly took the lead, and, before I knew it, I was moved in with her. I had only known her a couple of weeks. Off and on that went on for about three years, but we split up after about six months. I got involved with other women and so did she. We kind of lost track of each other. It's been about 10 years since I've heard from her. The last I heard she went to Chicago.

"Then in 1978, I started a 12-year relationship. I first met her at a party that Olivia and I had. She had moved up here with her lover. Meanwhile, I was living at my parents' home with my daughter. It's not unusual for an Italian family to have four generations in one house.

"Anyway, I had known this woman for a couple of years when we ran into each other one night down at one of the clubs. We went out together, and I moved in with her. God, that was a habit! I moved in with her and left my daughter with my folks. That lasted 12 stormy years.

"In retrospect, one can understand why. We have motivations that have nothing to do with the other person. At the time I thought things were fine, but when I look back . . . we were smoking dope and drinking some . . . doing all that stuff. She was out of town two weeks out of each month because she traveled for a company. So, in essence, we only saw each other six months out of the year.

"My lover was 20 years older than I was. I can look back now and see issues with my mom that I was acting out with her. It's funny when you hit your forties . . . things start to happen.

"I just didn't feel good about anything. I would have affairs while we were a couple. Even with my ex-husband. He was the only man I felt safe having sex with—both disease-wise and psychologically. The crazy thing was I never really liked it. It was weird. I can see now that I didn't know what I was doing. What brought this woman and I together couldn't keep us together any longer. It was painful.

"What caused it to end was that my mother died. When my mother got ill, my dad had died and she was living alone. My lover suggested that it would be a great idea for us to get a house and have Mom live with us. I had this relationship with my mom that was love-hate, but I did it, anyway, and Mom moved in downstairs. I got the feeling that my lover was manipulating all of this, and I was operating out of guilt.

"When my mom died, that did it. I knew my life was going to change. When I finally decided I had to change my life, our relationship changed. I tried to get my lover to go into therapy so she could understand that. I wanted her to understand that we shouldn't be together any longer. That was the coward's way out, and it was pretty stormy. So that was it.

"Meanwhile, Dwayne and I would talk about all this a lot. He always wanted to know what was happening. To this day, he is an interesting fellow. I could talk to him about anything. He is still around. He has been married for the last 12 years, but we are all together for family holidays. That may seem strange, but there is no reason for any animosity or jealousy with his wife because she knows I'm gay, and I'm no threat to her.

"It was good for my daughter because she never had parents that hated each other. My daughter is 26 now. I told her I was lesbian when she was 12. She told me she had known since she was 10!

"I think my daughter has had a pretty good sense of herself. I wanted to do for her what I really didn't get from my mom. I just wanted to nurture her and give her a sense of herself so she could move out on her own and not do what I did. She is a successful Ford model and she's doing just fine. She's had relationships with women, but she's straight. She thinks the soul is the soul. The body's just a vehicle. She says if she meets someone with whom there is a connection, she doesn't care what body it's in. She's not married and is very career oriented.

"The change-over was really bizarre in that I had none of the problems that a lot of women have; I mean, I embraced it. I'd even talk about it with all my friends. I never had a problem with the straight world. I think it was because I was comfortable with myself, and I didn't have any hangups about it. To me it was an adventure. This was 1969 and 1970. Those were the years when the thing to do was to know a gay person! It was all right. It was like coming home for me. It fit.

"I have a sister, and we were as different as night and day. I was the wild black sheep of the family. My sister was very conservative—married an FBI man.

"I never talked about it with my dad. All my friends would come over and Mom was like a surrogate mom to them. I secretly think my mom was a lesbian; I really do. My whole family knew. My grandmother, who was the matriarch, said, 'It's not who you are, it's what's inside here that counts.' What she said went in the family.

"I'm currently sort of in a relationship. When my mom died, I had to find out what was going on. So I started therapy. It turned out to be a lesbian therapist, although I didn't know it at the time. She has very strong boundaries. It's true . . . when you are ready the teacher appears; the connection was there. The therapy has been absolutely wonderful, and it's also the hardest thing I've ever done in my life.

"My issue was not my lesbianism. It was all the other issues. Just in the past five years, I have recalled that I was abused by uncles and by boys across the street. I was very sexually precocious. You suppress the abuse, I guess. I didn't turn to drugs or alcohol. I was lucky; I think it was the nurturing from my grandma. I always had to be in control and you can't be if you're drunk.

"Sex was almost like a drug to me, but I'd feel funny afterwards. I love women, but I don't hate men. I don't consider myself a separatist, but if there were no more men left in the world it wouldn't bother me.

"I truly believe that this is what I chose to do this lifetime— this experience. For the past two years I've been living single. I did meet somebody a year and a half ago. It was an immediate attraction. We didn't do the same old lesbian thing. Have you heard the joke about how you tell a lesbian on the second date? She drives up in a U-Haul!

"There is a lot to be said about the old saying that a long courtship is the best courtship. Two years . . . hey, that's nothing. It gives you time for the masks to come down. So that's what we've been doing. We have kind of seen other people in between. We have redefined the relationship.

"I'm not ready for a marriage. I'm just now discovering what I want in a relationship. I want to be claimed. I want to be treasured. Sex is fine, but I can't have sex to have sex anymore. I did a lot of that. "When I came out, there must have been 20 bars here in Seattle. Down in the square you could park your car and go all night. Because we were the baby-boomers, we were the largest population of gay women. It was a new phenomenon. It was unbelievable. You didn't have to worry about disease. I met the women at bars and parties. You can meet women anywhere. I meet 'em at Larry's Market, for God's sake. Nordstom's make-up counter downtown. That's the best place! The only difference is that you do safe sex now.

"I have been president of the Aurora Avenue Merchants Association for the past four years. The difference between now and 20 years ago is that I don't come out and say I'm gay. I'm just who I am, and it's never come up. They think I'm a liberal when I defend the gay men on Broadway. I have devoted the last two years to some introspection and have been living off of my investments. I got tired of the money thing. I like money; don't get me wrong. If most people knew how simple it was to make, they wouldn't work for anybody else.

"I have never had dreams before. I never wished upon a star when that song was out. Now I'm coming into who I am. I want to continue to do what I'm doing. I truly live in the moment now and that's a wonderful feeling. I have a connection I've never had before with the world. I want to embrace everything. My life is so different, because now there is no chaos or conflict.

"I want to have a partner someday. I know exactly what I want—the soul part of it. I want serenity. I want to be a whole person so I can be a whole person with somebody else. I want to explore some of the talents I've discovered that I have. Everybody always thought I had it all together. Now, I believe in more of my talents than I did before.

"I'm letting the spirituality happen in me. I have come to a place with my spirituality that I have peace and serenity. I think there will be a balance; I can have spirituality and also make money at the same time.

"I've discovered that I can write. I want to get back into the theater, or—in the production end of it. Back in high school I won the best actress award and won a scholarship to the Pasadena Playhouse, but I never did anything about it because I was too scared. I would really like to get involved in that again.

"I manifest what I want. I hope I come back next time as a lesbian, too. I'm having so much fun."

Pat

*I did the perfunctory things like trying to have a boyfriend.
Really, that just bored me to tears.*

Pat is 59. She was born in Texas. She has a M.A. in political science.
She works in a public school system.

"I just came out five years ago at the age of 55. I was married
twice.

"The first time I was married was for five years and my
husband died. Then I was single about a year and a half and
now have been legally married for something like 28 years. At
the time I came out, my mother was living with us and we
didn't want to split up housekeeping. It's been five years now,
and my mother still lives there with him. I didn't see any sense
in forcing any kind of change.

"One of the reasons I stayed with him so long is that he is
a real nice person. My lover and myself spend holidays with
him. I have an adopted daughter which he has also unofficially
adopted. There are no problems. He feels pretty comfortable
being in the same room with us. He knows I'm a lesbian. He
was the first person I told.

"I wrote him this long letter saying that all of our problems,
of which we had plenty, were just as much my doing as his. I
told him that I had decided for sure that I was a lesbian. I then
talked to him and he got up from the table and put his arm
around me and asked me how he could help me. It's kind of
hard to hate somebody who is so supportive.

"My daughter has always been very supportive, and, in
fact, she had a friend in high school who was a lesbian. It wasn't
any big deal to her. She is grown now with children of her own.

"I probably always knew I was a lesbian. I remember
myself as a small child and growing up. I did the perfunctory
things like trying to have a boy friend. Really, that just bored
me to tears. I wasn't very successful at it either. I really didn't

understand how all these girls were getting all that excited over these stupid guys. I was the perennial tomboy and played sandlot softball and all that. My mother made me quit at the appropriate age.

"When I went away to college I thought I would find out about all this. I read all the time so I knew something about homosexuals. The high school library books had told me that homosexuals were sick people and that they had to be cured. So I said, 'Not for me!' I went to college at a girls' school—it is jokingly referred to now as 'the dyke factory of Texas.' I totally avoided women who I knew were homosexuals. I set myself up with straight people.

"Then it became unbearable, and I began drinking. My folks were pillars of the community and the Methodist Church. My mother was very much the Southern belle and my father was the son of Yankees who'd moved to Texas. He was a Union man—so he was a little more radical. I was heavily into doing what my parents approved of. I felt they would be disappointed if I turned out to be one of those homosexuals. I never felt that I could talk to them. That first year of college was 1947. If I'd been less inclined to get information from books, I'd have probably been better off. I continued drinking to keep a lid on it . . . until five years ago, when I stopped drinking and came out.

"The reason I eventually made the decision to come out was because I visited an old high school friend whom I was crazy about. We exchanged confidences about our lives and I told her how miserable I was. She told me that she thought I ought to see a psychologist. I had seen that she had received good help from the feminist psychologist that she recommended. I went into therapy with her for six months and decided to quit drinking and to come out.

"My first experience with a woman was with that high school friend. It was a very brief and not a very satisfactory sort of thing that wasn't terribly wonderful, but it certainly didn't discourage me. I launched on with a vengeance. I proceed to try to get into every social group I could in order to meet people. I had four or five partners prior to my present partner.

I thought of each in terms of a long-term relationship. I was raised that way and I agree with it also.

"I finally got to the point of coming out to my husband and my mother. My mother is the sort of a person who doesn't deal with things. I told her that I was a lesbian and I was moving. She stayed with my husband and that was that.

"Moving out and being around other gays was an important decision for me. I got a little job working two hours a day at the Gay Political Caucus. Even though this was mostly gay men, I felt I could identify with them certainly more than I had even been able to identify with straight men. They would say little things about when they were children and I could understand. I gradually began to meet more and more women. I didn't join a lesbian group until a little later. I thought they were just a bunch of old women and I didn't want to get into that. I was probably more afraid of them because I did a lot of chasing of young women. That was to give myself more confidence, but it was remarkably unsuccessful!

"I am out with two of my former co-workers—only with people I feel comfortable with. For all I know everybody at work already knows. I'm fairly well-known politically. I don't know that they don't know, but I don't feel threatened in this job. I did not go back into teaching because I wanted to be out and I didn't want to have to deal with parents. In a few years, I hope to have a private practice in drug and alcohol abuse or hold some elective office, if I have the stamina to do it. I would be an openly gay candidate.

"I think women contemplating a change in lifestyle related to sexual preference should evaluate their feelings very carefully. They should read all they can and talk with others about lesbian lifestyles. They should look at themselves and see what would make them happiest. Go with their feelings. Also if they are doing any drinking or drugging, they ought to quit it because they can't understand their own feelings unless they are sober.

"I can add that I came out when I was 55 years old and I'm almost 60 now. I can say that these past five years have been the happiest years of my life. They haven't always been the easiest and I've had a lot of problems establishing a long-term relationship. I had some wonderful counseling and help along the way.

"This was the best decision of my life!"

Claire

At first I thought I wasn't a lesbian—I was just very attracted to this woman!

Claire is 43. She was born in Memphis, Tennessee. She has a B.A. in history and languages, a bachelor of music, and is a classical guitarist. She also has an A.A. degree in nursing and works as an operating room nurse.

"I was married only once, and once was enough! I have no children.

"My marriage was kind of a curious situation because I married my psychiatrist. We actually got married after I had been his mistress for years. The reason I got into therapy to begin with, as a 19-year old, was because I felt strange. I felt like I didn't fit in. I felt that something was wrong but I didn't know what it was. I went to college, but I didn't feel drawn to date boys.

"I didn't feel I knew the emotions that other people were talking about. I felt odd and I didn't know why. I couldn't seem to cope with the world. I went to college and I would make A's and would get terribly afraid and drop out. I told my parents that I just felt desperate, and so, I went into therapy. As it ended up, we never really addressed the issues. We got involved sexually shortly after my 21st birthday.

"I felt it was a fairly good and interesting relationship. He was 28 years older than I. I thought maybe the problem had been that I just didn't get along with young men. I thought I had a problem relating to men my age. After I got divorced and came out and got into therapy again, I started discovering that our relationship should never have happened.

"When I look back on it, it was not a good relationship for a number of reasons. I was 28 when we got married in 1978. He was very domineering—and an alcoholic. When I was married, I have to say, I was an alcoholic and I smoked a lot of

147

marijuana. After I got divorced, I thought my problem with it would stop, but it didn't. So then I realized I had a big problem with getting numb—with having to stay numb. So I got into therapy, and I'm good now. I got over it and I'm amazed at what it feels like not to be numb.

"Now I drink very little. I made a contract as to how much I would drink. I have only two glasses of wine and only when I'm out with people. I haven't even maxed out on that. No marijuana now.

"So, it was an abusive relationship, both mentally and sexually. He had the advantage and he didn't mind using it. He would have too much to drink and start out on a tirade about women. He had a lot of issues about his mother sending him off to a very strict private school in England. He never said anything nice about his mother. He would get on these tirades and he would talk for hours, just saying all the terrible things he could think of about women. I thought that no one had ever shown him what love was and I tried and tried and then I thought . . . whoa. This is getting nowhere; this is a lost cause.

"Then, during the last year of our marriage, something made me realize that I had been noticing women all my life. I realized that I paid them more attention than I had paid to men. It wasn't anything in particular that made me start thinking about that. Part of it was that Frank was more and more sexually abusive, and I got to thinking where my interest had been all along. Because he was a psychiatrist, I talked to him about the fact that I might be sexually interested in women. I thought I was bi-sexual. He was more interested in saying that he and I should have an open relationship sexually, which meant to him that he should be free to do what he wanted with other women.

"Then, Frank was making plans to retire to a town in Florida, and I moved there a year ahead of him. I realized that I had looked forward to being away from him and living by myself for awhile. In that year I started to really think about myself and what was going on. At that point, he wrote to me that he had gotten sexually involved with a patient. That's when I began to know that something was really wrong.

"In the meantime, I was very much attracted to a certain woman. But, when I talked to Frank about it, he wanted the three of us to get involved. I got very mad because I felt that he wanted to take everything away from me. So I said, 'No, I'm not going to get involved with you and another woman.' Then, I began to focus on women rather than denying that I had been more interested and more emotionally drawn to women all my life.

"These new feelings seemed perfectly natural to me. I did not know any lesbians; yet, I knew I could love women in a heartbeat. I didn't know I was a lesbian. From the pictures that the culture painted of lesbians, I thought that they were a very hard, rough bunch of tough women with tattoos and leather and butch haircuts driving trucks. So I thought, from that, that I wasn't a lesbian. I just happened to be very attracted to this woman; but I'm not a lesbian. I'm not one of them!

"This woman that I was so attracted to was a woman working at the same place as I. Her husband also worked there and was putting the moves on me. I kept telling him, 'No.' and, 'Get away from me.' His wife was someone I really liked. I wanted her to be a good friend of mine . . . and, yes, I found her terribly attractive. I wasn't attracted to him at all, but he was very sharp. He figured it out—that I was hot for his wife, which I was. He lied to me and said, 'She really likes you. You ought to come to our house and spend some time with us.' Actually, he wanted to get in bed with me. He wanted to get in bed with anything that moved.

"My first sexual encounter with a woman was with the two of them, and I realized during that episode that I was crazy about her and had no feelings about him. The terrible truth of that was that he had lied about his wife. She really was not interested and really wanted nothing to do with it. I left that experience feeling really used and stupid. But it did confirm for me that my emotional pull was toward women.

"Later, that woman went out to lunch with me one day because she wanted to talk to me. She said, 'I don't know what is going on but I find you so incredibly attractive.' She just told me that she was so attracted to me. I said, 'Fine. I'm delighted that you are and I don't find that odd at all.' Nothing ever came of it, though I would have welcomed it. She was not able to think about anything more than being around each other and being close friends. We have stayed good friends, and recently we got together and talked about what happened between us in 1986. She now says that she isn't interested in sex with anyone.

"I've had two lesbian relationships. The first woman had been a friend of mine when I was married and had been a very closeted lesbian. I was still, at that time, a lesbian virgin. I had decided that I had better look into this situation. I went to a women's music festival outside of Atlanta in 1987 with this closeted friend and another woman. Eventually, my friend and I were involved for a couple of years.

"Then I moved to another town in Florida where there was a women's community. I went to some of their social events and was learning how to make contacts. I met my second partner there. We had what I thought was going to be a long-term relationship, but it only lasted three years, ending a year ago. We had thought that it was going to be a pretty committed relationship, but it was a very painful breakup. We weren't getting along very well the last year, and I finally realized that I had quit loving her. Then, I decided to move out here. I am not currently in a relationship.

"I am not exactly closeted. I decided that when it would occur naturally, I would let people know. I would be honest. As I make new friends, and the discussion comes up, I tell people where I stand. I share a house right now with two straight people I work with, and it hasn't come up that I should have to explain my lifestyle to them.

"I had made this agreement with myself that I wanted to be closer to my family. All the time that I was married, my husband had had this successful campaign to drive a wedge between me and my family. I've gradually tried to make better ties with my family after I got divorced. So, at Christmas time, I was taking a walk with my mother and the subject of homosexuality came up. I came out to her then, and she was the most

150

wonderful person in the world. My mother is 70, and she was wonderful about it.

"I didn't talk to my father, as he's always been the difficult one for me to talk to. At any family discussions all during my life, my father and I have been at odds. He is not the open-minded kind of person that my mother is.

"I have an older brother who lives in California. I called him up one time when I was pretty lonesome. He had met one of my partners earlier when we went on a trip to California. At the time of the call he said, 'Well, isn't she with you?' I said, 'No, Frank, I better explain that to you.' So I explained to him that she and I had been more than just friends and that I had broken up with her and had moved here by myself. He said, 'Hey. O.K. Whatever you do is your business. It just seems like you've picked a really difficult lifestyle.' I told him that it wasn't more difficult than trying to be something I'm not.

"I've since been to see my brother and we had a wonderful visit, the closest visit that we've ever had. I have a younger brother who doesn't know a lot about me. He is a fundamentalist-born-again-kind-of-guy. My younger sister and I get along fine, and it just hasn't come up. If it does I'll tell her.

"Sometimes, I find that it's a pressure to not come out. It's enough of a pressure to create a lot of stomach acid. Sometimes, I think, in maintaining secrecy, I feel that I'm about to burst. Sometimes, I think it's not worth it. I just haven't found the ideal way to do it.

"I had a friend back in Florida where I was working and she figured out about me on her own. She just said something to me one day—without using the L word—that let me know that she knew I was in a significant relationship with a woman. In my working relationships, it creates some distance between me and the straight people I work with.

"To be a lesbian feels like a natural thing for me. I have a little problem wondering if I'm fitting into the lesbian community. Sometimes I feel a little intimidated by people who have always known they were lesbians. For me, it's just been since 1987. That is one reason I picked this area to move to because it's supposed to have a large women's community. I live with a straight couple, so my next move is going to be either to share housing with people in the gay community or to just move on my own and associate more with women in the gay community.

"I've been here nine months and I've met a few people who now feel like old friends. Five years from now I think I'll still be in this area. I see making some changes with what I want to do with my nursing career. I'd like to make a nice salary. I work in an operating room and wouldn't it be wonderful if I could find a lesbian surgeon to work with in a collaborative way? However, I'm not going to be worried about chasing down the perfect relationship. I'm going to let that happen when it happens. I would like to be in a committed relationship.

"When I was first coming out, I was really afraid of lesbians. And I was certainly afraid of not being accepted. My fear was that I would discover that I wasn't really interested in men, and, yet, the women I might turn to would reject me . . . then where would I be? I would be totally out in the cold.

"What I did was go to this women's festival and when I was there I looked around and saw all these women—I saw no men. I think the best thing to do is go to a place where there are no men.

"Go to a safe place, and see women taking care of themselves and associating with each other. Going to that festival was the greatest thing for me because I realized it could be done. Our culture wants to divide us and keep us apart. It is scary to turn our backs on the men in control. The festival was wonderful just to see all that group of lesbians providing support for each other."

Lynn

*My advice for women who are thinking about being a
lesbian is to go for it. . . . There are so many of us who are
out, it's not as scary as it used to be. . . . It's the best form of
love anybody can have.*

Lynn is 44. She is currently working on a doctorate in social welfare.

"I was married in 1969 for 16 years. It was a long time. I was
21; he was 24. I lived in Minneapolis.

"At the time, I remember having lots of feelings about
getting married. Mostly, I had a sense of relief that I would
have something to do with my life. My home situation was not
abusive or terribly painful, but there were enough tensions
there that marriage was an escape. I had no sense of being
passionately in love. I remember thinking, 'Well, he's not so
bad.'

"It seemed like kind of a fresh start for me. I hadn't had
much success in deciding what to do with my life, and it
seemed to me that this was my chance to do something that had
a chance for success. I had done a little dating of men, and I
certainly had no conception of what being a lesbian was about.
I just knew I wasn't like that.

"I don't think I gave the marriage much thought. I just
thought I would do what I had to do and that would be that.
There were times during the marriage when I felt very content,
but, mostly, I felt oppressed. I would say that the years that my
kids were little were the most tension-free times of my marriage. The children took up my life and gave me a purpose. But
after awhile, I felt like I was in a tomb. I thought I would die
unless I got out. It didn't have to do with sexuality, but rather,
with my sense that there was no substance to my life. My
religious upbringing said to me that I ought to be doing
something more with my life. I had a kind of guilt about that.

153

"At that time, and up until my divorce, I was involved in a very conservative fundamentalist religion. I did a lot of work with women's groups, one of which was a Christian feminist group. As a result of this group, one of the things I was being exposed to in my reading was the whole notion of loving women. That was the turning point for me. I began to see that, to me, the issue in feminism was whether or not you could totally love women. Then the question became was there any point which you could say, 'I won't love women?' And that meant sexual love as well.

"Finally, I threw out everything about morality that I had been taught and decided that to be committed as a feminist to women meant *loving women*. I then needed to find some confirmation from some other source. I had heard about this book called, *Is the Homosexual My Neighbor?*, and I remember being afraid of reading that book. I knew it would tell me it was all O.K. When I bought it and read it, it dispelled every notion I'd ever had about what the Bible says. At that point, I felt like I was open to anything. However, I didn't make the choice to be a lesbian . . . yet.

"When I turned 35 and my youngest went into the first grade, I made the big break and I went back to school. I hadn't been in school more than a week when I promptly fell in love with a teacher—a female, of course. I was mad over her. She was one of the first radical feminists I had ever known. I knew she could teach me a lot, and I was open to a lot of different things. I was aware of my own feelings in a way that I had never been before. So, we developed a friendship. She was very careful not to turn it into a sexual relationship. If she had initiated anything at that time, I would have just been right there.

"So, I went through two years of being totally in love with her—but still married. I was realizing that I couldn't be everything I wanted to be and remain in my marriage. I had the undying hope that this teacher would decide she wanted me. At the same time, there was something that told me that that would never happen. I had to begin to make some decisions based on what I wanted my future to be and where my commitments were. So, I began thinking about my own sexuality and what I wanted.

"I realized that there was some part of me that just felt totally natural about being a lesbian, and that this was the decision that I had to make. I felt it was a political choice. To me it was the only choice for a feminist. I still can't imagine making any other decision.

"I saw a counselor during my divorce—for my divorce. She was a lesbian therapist. I've never had any counseling around my being lesbian. I wasn't tormented by it. I have never been ashamed or embarrassed or felt like a freak.

"In 1984, while still married, I had several close relationships. I had one friend who was going through a divorce and she was exploring different kinds of relationships. We were very close, but she never could deal with a physical relationship. I went to Boston for a conference and met a woman there to whom I was very attracted. We ended up spending a few days together and talking a lot. The opportunity came up for the two of us to be alone and we did have a sexual experience. That was the first sexual intimacy that I had with a woman.

"I remember thinking that I didn't know whether I could do it. I didn't know what I would think or whether I would like it. There was a part of me that was just watching to see how it would go. I thought, 'Well, I did that pretty well. I could probably make it as a lesbian!'

"That was when I told myself that I was going to be a lesbian. I was the one who did everything, and this other woman was grateful. It felt right to me in terms of trying on behaviors. I remember thinking at the time that I knew she and I would not have a relationship. For a few hours I was kind of star-struck and wondered about it, but it became clear to me that it wasn't going anywhere.

"When I came back from that conference I sought out my friend—the one who was going through the divorce—and I reported back from this Christian conference. I thought she would think it was funny, but when I told her, she just got these huge eyes and she excused herself and left. When she came back, I asked her where she went, and she told me that she had

155

gone into the bathroom and just screamed. She told me that she couldn't believe that I did that. I had never considered the enormity of it. I just did it, and it was fun. It felt like another step in my own growth. Anyway, she could not deal with it.

"A few days went by, and she came around, and we ended up becoming lovers for about four months. Then, she couldn't handle it anymore. She was going through a divorce, and she was also a recovering alcoholic, and she had started drinking again. She was in very bad shape in a lot of ways. I think her husband suspected that there was something going on between the two of us. My husband never did.

"Anyway, we were in that sort of relationship for about four months when she decided she couldn't handle it any more. We still remained friends but we stopped having any sexual relationship. During that time, I made a firm decision in my own mind that I was never ever going to have sex again with my husband unless I wanted it. That was the beginning of the end of our marriage. I became celibate and didn't have any relationships for a while. Then, I had another brief relationship with another student at the college I was attending. That was when the divorce started.

"I now have a wonderful relationship with Mary. I am very, very happy. I had known Mary since 1982. She lived here and I lived in Minneapolis. She and I belonged to the same Christian feminist organization. We knew each other because we were on the national board of the organization. One of the first feminist things I ever did was to come here to their national conference. I walked into the area and there was this blatant sign that said, 'Any lesbians and friends come to room so-and-so for a get-together.' I thought, 'Wow—this is really something! They could actually put the word *lesbian* in this message center.'

"Mary was the coordinator of that conference. It turns out that she was not out, and she had not even admitted the possibility to herself that she was a lesbian. So, we had known each other and kept meeting at these conferences, but we didn't actually get to know each other until 1984. When I got to know her, I was just totally impressed by her being. She is one of the most wise, compassionate, gracious women I have ever known. I had no conception of ever pursuing a relationship with her.

"Mary had told me that she would keep in touch, and she had been calling me every now and then during that year. I remember being totally dumbfounded that she would even think it was important to talk with me. The only time we had even seen each other was once a year for the last four years at these conferences. Then, by the next conference, I had moved out. My ex-husband had seen fit to give me only $200 a month, and I was trying to live on that.

"Mary called to see if I was going to the conference coming up in California. I told her I didn't think I could do it because I didn't have any money. She suggested I call someone to get some scholarship help, and she told me on the phone that she was really sorry that I was living in such poverty. She said that she really wanted me to come out to the coast because she wanted to tell me about something. She said, 'I am happier now than I have ever been in my whole life, and I want to tell you about it because I want to make some changes.' That's all she said, and then we hung up. I said to myself, 'Mary is a lesbian!' I just knew that that was what she was talking about.

"So, I went out to Fresno to the conference. I was in the airport and someone called my name. I hardly recognized this woman because she was so different. I realized it was Mary, and she looked wonderful to me. We gave each other a big hug. At this point, I had not said anything to her about my being a lesbian. So, when we got to the conference, I just decided that I was going to tell her. When I said that I was a lesbian, she just looked at me and started laughing. She said, 'You are? I am, too.' We were in this place surrounded by all these women and we just collapsed into each other's arms.

"We decided we didn't want to stay there anymore, so we took our food to the room and we just started talking about everything that had happened to both of us. We spent every minute of the conference together—four days.

"We drove up to an executive meeting at a private cabin in the mountains after the conference. I remember that I was so

157

calculating about the whole thing. I just knew that I wanted to be with her. When we got there, I dashed into the cabin and found the one room that just had one bed, and staked out that room. We had been together all day, and, by that night, we both knew that we wanted to be as close to each other as we could possibly be. I've always wondered how many lesbian couples date their anniversary to the first night they spend together.

"I still wasn't sure that that was the beginning of a relationship because we still lived in separate cities. And I still didn't know what I was going to be doing with my life. I had just graduated with my B.A. So I went back to Minneapolis having a lot of questions. I thought maybe it was another of my other brief relationships. But she called as soon as I got back, and she called every day. Then I started calling. We really got to know each other over the phone. I still wasn't sure I wanted a committed relationship. That seemed oppressive to me coming from a marriage. I was really torn for awhile, and it was hard being so far away.

"In the meantime, I was in this four-month relationship when Mary and I got together. I was out of the house and totally independent, and in the process of getting my divorce. I practically lived at Kristen's house, but I was beginning to chafe. I felt it wasn't quite what I wanted. I knew I couldn't stay with her the rest of my life, but I had so many things going on in my life that I didn't want to think of having to end that relationship and start another. Yet, when I got back from being with Mary, that's exactly what happened. I went through the process of ending the relationship with Kristen. We talked, and it was O.K.

"At the same time, there was this other woman, not Mary. Spirituality had become important to me. I'm much more aware about having impressions and intuitions about things. One of the things that I knew was going to happen was that this woman who I had known for a while—who I had met at a dance—would come back into my life. I was ending this relationship with Kristen, I was exploring beginning this relationship with Mary, and here is this other woman back in my life. For a few weeks, we had a sexual relationship. I guess I was

158

making sure I didn't leave any stones unturned! I had to be sure about this. I didn't want to wonder what it would have been like. Somehow, being with this other woman didn't seem right to me. I did a lot of living and experimenting in a very short time.

"Then, Mary came to Minneapolis to visit, and we talked it all out. I asked all of the questions I had been wanting to ask, one of which was how old she was. That was a real important thing to me. I knew that she was older than I was but I didn't know how much. When she told me, I almost dropped my teeth because I hadn't realized that she was that much older than me. She is another generation older than me—18 years older. It made me pause for a minute. Here was this woman who was almost as old as my mother. I'm just beginning a career and Mary is winding down hers.

"It was during that visit that I knew I wanted to be with her. I had started investigating graduate school at that time, and I started making arrangements to apply. One issue I had to work out was leaving my kids. I have two sons. They were with my husband, but I had always lived close to them. But when I thought about wanting to be in a relationship with Mary, there was no other option that I could think of. Mary's career was in the West. She was willing to do anything—to take early retirement and move to Minneapolis but somehow that didn't make any sense at all.

"I had been seeing a counselor for support going through the divorce, and I sought short-term counseling for me and my kids around my move. My kids know that I'm lesbian. When I had first moved out of the house, a friend had me house-sit for her, and my two sons could come to stay with me. One of the times they came over we went for a walk; they were 10 and 13. I told them that I was a lesbian and what that meant about loving women, and they didn't say a word. So I let it lie at that point. My youngest son always takes things in stride. He finally said that he didn't care what other people say, and he didn't care what I was. My other son has always been much more reticent talking about my being a lesbian. They both let me know in their own way over the years that it was O.K. with them.

"My oldest just turned 19 and he is a freshman in college now. My youngest son is 15. They both live in Minnesota with their father. When we were divorced he got physical custody but we had joint legal custody. That whole custody situation is one that is very painful for me. It's probably the one area in my life where I still feel very powerless and oppressed by the system. My ex-husband got custody because he insisted on it. Basically what he said was that if I didn't agree to that he would fight me with every penny that he had, which was considerably more money than I had. I had no income, as I wasn't working then.

"My sons have met Mary and they like her. They have come out to visit ever since I moved. My youngest son has spent the most time because he was 10 when I moved out here. Now as he is getting older he is more involved in his own life. They both are still out here at least twice a year.

"My mother knows I am a lesbian. She is a very conservative, 'closeted' mother. I am very open about being a lesbian everywhere I've always been, and telling people that I'm a lesbian is not an issue for me. But talking to her was the most frightening thing I ever did. I didn't have any idea what her reaction would be. But it was everything I could have hoped for. She said it was my decision and that she didn't love me any less. She doesn't understand it, especially the political part. We have a good relationship. She knows Mary and likes her. My mom has just recently gotten married for the third time. I have no idea what she has said to her new husband; I haven't met him.

"I'll finish this doctorate within the next year. I want to combine writing and advocacy, and I want to work with women. I'm not sure what that means yet. I'm not sure I will make my career in Social Work. I doubt it. I'd love to get an interesting position in Women's Studies. I dream about having a little bed and breakfast somewhere for women, and we've talked about having a retreat center.

"My advice for women who are thinking about lesbianism is go for it! The decision is not the scary sort of decision that it used to be. There are so many of us who are out. There is a formidable power that has been unleashed. It's the best form of love anybody can have."

Susan

We were married for 21 years. . . . Then I fell
in love with a woman!

Susan is 51. She has degrees in speech pathology and audiology, and
a B.S. degree in nursing. She works in oncology nursing.

"When I met Tom I was 17 and a freshman in college, and
we went together from then on. We were engaged for five years
and got married. We were married for 21 years and had three
children. Then I fell in love with a woman!

"Without naming it or thinking of what was going on, it
just happened. It was an intense friendship at first and then I
started to realize that there was something going on that was
sexual, too. It was exciting and it was scary. It was scary in that
I didn't know what was going to happen next either in that
relationship or in my whole life with my husband and children.

"Actually, Tom and I were in a class that Chris was teaching. It was a group that she was doing at the church at which
she was a minister, and some friends of ours, a couple, asked
us if we would like to join them at the class. It was in the days
when everybody had personal growth groups and that kind of
thing. We went and it was a very good group.

"There was just a special spark that went between Chris
and me. I felt very interested in having a friendship with her.
She was someone I had heard a lot about for some time before
I met her. This friend of mine who brought us to class was a part
of her church and thought a great deal of her. At that point it
never occurred to me to have sexual thoughts about another
woman. I just thought that this was someone I really wanted to
be friends with.

"So, after the class finished, she and I got together a couple
of times for coffee and later had a picnic with my youngest
child. We did a few things like that, then she went to England

162

for the summer. Her parents were living there. We had a little correspondence while she was in England and it was particularly intense. When she came back we spent a lot of time together. Very gradually it evolved into a sexual relationship. "I never had the feeling that I didn't want to be a lesbian. Before long I was able to name it. We both kind of looked at each other and said, 'Do you know what this means?' It's not like we were pretending that we didn't know what we were doing. We were both 33, and neither one of us had ever been with a woman before.

"I told Tom what we were doing—not knowing what his reaction was going to be—and he responded that maybe he needed to get to know Chris better, too. She had been spending a lot of time with all of us as a family. Then he spent some time with her on his own, and they started a sexual relationship. So that was the way it was when she moved in. It was about six months after we had started to become close. All three of us didn't go to bed together at the same time, but there were sexual relationships going among our different couples. We were not into being a threesome—in bed—or really any place else. We were a collection of couples. This is the craziest thing that I have ever done in my life.

"I'm sort of glad I did something totally crazy. Now I can relate to others who do crazy things. When we all look at it now, we say, 'How could we have been so dumb or so naive to think we could make anything like that work?' It didn't. I was with her the five years she lived there. You know, the beauty of it was that we all managed to stay good friends, too. After a few years, when it had all split up, Chris and I started to rebuild our friendship and now we are the very best of friends. Tom and Chris don't really see each other, although there is no hostility between them.

"Tom and I are good friends. All the things that were good in our relationship survived the divorce. We always treated each other with respect. There still is a lot of affection there, and I consider him a part of my family. My kids are my closest family and I have one sister with whom I'm very close. I have a good relationship with them. I also have my close friends who are my chosen family.

"I had one other relationship with a man after I had had that relationship with Chris. And there were four relationships with women. The shortest one was 18 months. Every relationship with a woman has lasted at least that long although I haven't lived with each one. One was a long distance relationship with a woman in California. She was an old P.E. teacher of mine who I had got back in touch with and we had a relationship going. We'd get together every six weeks or so and we'd take trips together but I knew that it was going absolutely nowhere.

"I was working nights and I didn't see how I was ever going to meet anybody. I had no inroads into the lesbian community. I had finished school and then was working nights and had this long distance relationship going. I was looking at what I might do, including going to some lesbian resource center groups. I knew I had to do something, not even so much that I wanted an intimate relationship—I just needed to know some other lesbians. The only lesbians I knew were two former lovers and they didn't seem to be very interested in introducing me to any of their friends. Each one of those relationships had been pretty closeted and I never felt like I knew other lesbians.

"Then one day I happened to pick up a copy of *The Weekly*, where the ads are, and there was a real cute ad and that's how I met the person with whom I had my next relationship. I did meet more people through her; she had more friends and was a little more into the community than I had ever been before.

"I have never liked to go to bars to meet people. I like to do things in the outdoors—I like to go up in the mountains and go hiking and that kind of thing. I also really love to go to the theater—plays and concerts. I also like hanging out by myself and puttering around. I get in a bad way if I don't have enough time of my own. I spend time alone just being relaxed and refreshed.

"I am currently in a relationship with Sharon. I met her at work when I was taking care of her mother. I found her to be

164

a really interesting and attractive person—it was certainly her eyes. I just knew in my mind that she was a lesbian, and a friend of mine who is a social worker said Sharon was a lesbian and had a partner. She didn't know about me—people don't usually know about me.

"So, I was looking on her as a lesbian. I remember wondering, 'Why don't I get to meet people like this?' I could imagine meeting another nurse but a patient's family member—I had never thought of that as a possibility. I remember wishing I could have a friend like this in my life. I was thinking she was very attractive and about the right age. I was also very interested in what she was doing with her life. She was making a major career change and she talked about it in such an animated way. That was something I had done too and I could really relate to it. She had a lot of good energy. She was just very open and friendly. My feelings were just, Gee! What a shame she was taken.

"I had to call her the night I thought her mother was going to die to say that she should get in to the hospital soon. I got her answering machine and I remember thinking afterwards that the message on the machine seemed as if only one person lived there. But people do have relationships where they don't live together.

"I did then take a really unusual step for me; I reached out to her when she left that night, saying to her, 'I think I'm going to see you again and that we may have more in common than you realize.' That was sort of mysterious thing for me to say to her. I figured that she had no idea that I was a lesbian.

"I knew I wouldn't call her, and I really didn't think she'd call me. I thought I might run in to her sometime at some lesbian concert or something like that. That has happened to me where I have run in to family members of patients in public places. There is this instant recognition of, 'Oh my God, I didn't know you were one too.' That's what I thought would happen with Sharon. I told people about her. I told my daughter that I had met this person who was neat but that was kind of the end of it. Then Sharon called me.

"She had figured what I meant about 'more in common than you realize.' It went really rather quickly after that. She was not involved with anyone, and we started out by just doing some things together. But, both of us were around 50 when we met, and we knew what kind of relationship we wanted. It became clear to both of us that this was it.

"We moved very quickly into making plans for being together and we had our commitment ceremony after we had known each other a little over a year. We wanted to move quickly into living together, but we won't do that until the house I have now is remodeled and she sells the house she in living in. We've known all along that that's what we were going to do. We both have a lot of confidence that this is going to be the relationship that we both go out on.

In many ways Sharon was just what I wanted and needed. I had had a lot of unsuccessful relationships that I got into for the wrong reasons and in the wrong way. I had at that point gone through therapy and I got out of a relationship that I needed to end. For the first time ever I was single and was happy being single. I wasn't looking for a relationship at all. I also knew that if I ever did have another relationship, it was going to be the right one. I just didn't want to get into one just to be in one. I just had a sense that this was the right one.

"I found a journal the other day that I had written shortly after meeting Sharon and I saw where I was already thinking about having a ceremony. I thought then that this relationship was going to be the big one. I had never even wanted to live with any other woman with whom I had had a relationship. Fortunately, she was ready too.

"I feel really challenged by Sharon and that was one of the things I really needed. I guess that was what was missing from before. She really wants to work on our relationship and our communication. She is really honest and pushes me to be. Before, it always seemed I was the one who had to do those things and that's not the case any more. Also, we are different in a lot of ways. That's good too. We complement each other. It's exciting. I would not get into another relationship again unless I felt that way. I would not be bored just for a relationship. Being alone would be much, much better.

"I was totally closeted during the early years. It was not difficult for me personally, but I thought it was difficult socially. It was certainly complicated by the fact that I was married and had three small children. Our attitude toward our children was that we would never lie to them but we didn't force any information on them either. They asked questions when they were ready. The year would have been about 1973. I may as well have been on the moon because I had this relationship, but we were not part of any community at all. What I was doing was beyond the pale because the three of us were living together. My husband and I didn't feel we would be safe exposing that to anybody.

"I guess the only place where I'm not out now is at work. But, I know my job would not be threatened if I came out there. There are a lot of gay nurses where I work, and there is no threat. I just haven't felt it was important to do. There is one person at work who knows. The rest have known me for six years and never known this about me. So now I feel I would be making some grand announcement. If someone else made the announcement—I wouldn't mind if they knew.

"My daughter is a lesbian, and she and other young lesbians I know are very, very comfortable with being who they are and are very supported in their work and social environments. I haven't ever really seen that they have felt the kind of discrimination that older lesbians have. They have come out in a totally open and supportive environment—like my daughter. She came out when she was in college and it was wonderful to be a lesbian. There was no question about coming out. She continues to live her life pretty much that way whereas for me coming out to straight friends—it is a process that has taken me some time and I'm still not out at work.

If I could live my life over again I wouldn't do it differently. I wouldn't have had my children if I had done things differently and they are a very important part of my life. Not having them is unimaginable. From the point of view of my own fulfillment and my own self-development, I don't think I ever really felt like I knew myself or felt attractive before I knew I was a lesbian. I think that there was something that just wasn't quite right and I didn't know what it was for all those years. I like who I am now and I got here because of all the things that went before. I've got the best of two worlds.

Five years from now—I really look forward to five years from now—I think I will still be working. I'm an oncology nurse now. I went back to school when I was in my forties. I have a B.S. in speech pathology and a master's degree in audiology. I used to be a speech pathologist, but I'd been out of the field for a really long time and I didn't have any passion for going back into doing it. I wanted to do something that I really had some passion about doing. I felt free to make a clean choice at that time and really do what I wanted to do. So I went back to school and got a B.S. in nursing.

"I've been a nurse for seven years and I really like it. It is such hard work that I might decide that I've had enough of it. I'm not close to burning out, although it is physically and mentally hard. I expect that I will still be working, but probably half time.

"I really look forward to that time because by then Sharon and I will have gone through some of the rough parts of living together. I think both of us feel that there will be a lot of adjusting to do.

"We are very strong people and kind of set in our ways. But we don't have any doubt that we will be able to work it out."

Binnie

*What worked for me in this change of sexual orientation
was to keep an open heart and mind.*

Binnie is 34. She was born in Seattle, Washington. She graduated
from cosmetology school and is a cosmetologist.

"I wasn't quite 14 when I left home. My mother was an
alcoholic and has been married five times. It was a very abusive
home life. By that time my mother was on her fourth marriage,
and the abuse with the stepfather was horrendous. I told my
mother that it was either him or me and so—I left home.

"I moved up to Vancouver at that point and lived there for
several years. I was on my own. I got myself through school
and I was a topless dancer. That's where I met my husband,
Steve. He was from the States and came up with some friends.
He came to the club where I was dancing. We were married for
roughly seven years. The last two years it was kind of on and
off.

"On the whole, our marriage was a kind of healing process
more than anything. He was six years older than I was. He was
kind and gentle and I was pretty calloused. It was hard for me
to show affection. I wasn't trusting. Steve had the capability of
working through some things with me.

"To this day, I look back and see that he was a wonderful
man. We kind of just grew apart. He had dreams and ideas. By
the time I was in my mid-twenties I was not going the same
direction he was. We parted friends. I saw him up until four or
five years ago. He finally remarried. He wanted children really
bad which was not my cup of tea. He remarried and he had
twin boys and that was good for him.

"My mother had a relationship with a woman when I was
young. That time was probably one of the best times for me and
my brother. Things were serene! I would want to go home
instead of not wanting to go home. I remember wondering in

169

the back of my mind what this bond was. I wondered how things could be so calm in my mother's chaotic life.

"Shortly after Steve and I actually split up, I was still living here on the island and tending bar. I knew a lot of lesbian women around here. I was never intimidated or shy or afraid to say hello. I could have cared less. If they said hi back, that was great.

"I somehow got involved with a bunch of lesbian women. I played sports. For the first time in my life I had a lot of intimate, close women friends. I think a lot of women were intimidated by me before. I had always been bold and outspoken. I definitely have an opinion and I'm not afraid to speak it out. So it was always very hard for me to get close to women. I think I always wanted that but I didn't know how to go about it.

"Suddenly, I found myself with all these women. They would call and say, 'We are going down to Maxwelton and play softball. Why don't you come down?' I was suddenly accepted and was very content with the bonding and sharing that women have. That is kind of how it all got started. I think I was 25.

"In the midst of these gals, there was a single gal. She hadn't had a relationship in quite a few years and she was a good friend of my present partner. The next thing I know we were together. We shared about a year together—separate places, but it was during that time that Marty, another friend, was going through some problems with her partner. I don't know what really transpired between Marty and me, but Marty used to come into the bar where I worked.

"Now, this was a bar for retired types—a lot of retired gentlemen who had known me since I moved here when I was in my late teens. They kind of saw me grow up. And Marty would come in and would bring me flowers and sit at the end of the bar and just court me! Anyway, after about a year Cheryl and I broke up—I had to tell her that we had wonderful friendship but I wasn't in love. That's what I was looking for at the time. We split up but are still very good friends.

"I don't know how I can explain how I really feel about this. When I fell in love with Marty, it was like something I had never experienced in my life. It was—she charmed the socks right off of me. Eight years later I still love her to pieces. In fact, Marty and I didn't have a physical relationship for six months. Other than kissing, we just thought we would take it nice and slow. The whole time we spent—those six months—I never thought of her as being male or female. I never thought of her as being a sex. I just knew that I loved her. I knew that I had to be with her. So that was easy.

"I didn't have to rush out and see a shrink—I've never been to one. I was fortunate, too. I remember the first time my folks met Marty. Now my folks had met Charley and Cheryl and a lot of my lesbian friends. I did a lot of lip-synching for a place up in Everett for the Chicken Soup Brigade and other fund raising. My folks used to come watch me perform.

"Anyway, I can remember the first time on a Thanksgiving at my parents' home and Marty came. At that point I hadn't told my folks that Marty and I were planning on moving in together. It was no grandstand anything. I just said that I was bringing a friend over. Before the evening was over, my stepdad whispered to me, 'I don't think I've ever seen so much love that happens between two people as between the two of you.'

"We are both very fortunate in that we have families that love both of us and accept both of us. Marty is part of our family. I'm also a part of hers. They are totally aware of the relationship.

"I'm out with my brothers and sisters. Marty is a whole different story. She is a California girl. She found out early that she was lesbian and socialized with nothing but lesbian friends. She has a total of seven other brothers and sisters. They just accept that that is Marty.

"I have one brother who is three years younger than I am. He is kind of shy and doesn't say a lot, but the first time he met Marty he absolutely adored her. They are good friends. He knows about the relationship.

"I am out to all the people I work or worked with. I'm a beautician. I've done that for seven years. I love it. I even have clients who ask me why I don't have a boyfriend. And I say, 'Did you ask me because you really want to know?' And they'll say, 'Yeah,' and I tell them. I've very seldom had somebody, at least while they are in my chair, get up and leave or anything. In fact, this one gal who was in my chair not long ago says, 'O.K., you've been doing my hair for years and I want to know what it is with you and Marty.' I said that we had been living together for eight years. I said, 'Yes, we are together.' She says, 'Hot damn! I'm glad you told me that. It's been on my mind for a long time.'

"I have, however, lost clients that have found out through the community. I had a mother and daughter who I had been doing for about five years. In fact they followed me to this shop. Someone told them I was lesbian, and the daughter called me on the phone and told me that she could no longer come to me. Every time that happens it hurts.

"I have this dream that Marty and I are old and sitting on our front porch rocking in chairs. Marty will be finished with school. She has one more year. It's been a rough year with only one income. But we get through it O.K. We are definitely going to be building something on our property. We also talk about having a child. We'll probably adopt. We'll probably get a black child as Marty's parents adopted two black children and she was very close to them.

"We have also raised two children. When I first met Marty she had her 13-year-old brother with her. He was sent up here because he was incorrigible. He was failing school and into drugs and a dropout. We raised him from 13 until he graduated high school with honors. He is now in his third year of college. We didn't baby him; we just gave him rules that he had to abide by. We told him he was responsible for getting up to go to school. I don't know why it worked, it just worked!

"I also have a godson who is going to be 21 soon. I have had him off and on from when he was nine until he was 17. There were several years that overlapped that we had both kids in our home. Pretty wild!

"We have great fun together. We love camping. We ride bicycles. We are really into our animals. We have a dog that we take to the beaches. Sometimes we go to Seattle and walk around Pike Place Market. We both like to cook. I'm kind of a social butterfly so I love to entertain. I play music a little bit. Marty and I sing some; she has a beautiful voice.

"What worked for me in this change of sexual orientation was to keep an open heart and mind. I think honesty is something all of us could do with a little more of. It certainly isn't easy. It can be very lonely—living a double standard of life. I think that without honesty both lives aren't full. You are not living to the potential of what you could do.

"It would have been a lot lonelier if I hadn't been committed to honesty. I'm not lonely and I know that I can pick up the phone and call my mother. If I'm just feeling blue about something I can share that with her.

"I have a lot of people I can call upon. I think that's really important. We all need that."

Reference List

Periodicals

Common Lives/Lesbian Lives, A Lesbian Quarterly
P.O. Box 1553
Iowa City, IA 52244

Hot Wire, The Journal of Women's Music and Culture
Empty Closet Enterprises, Inc.
5210 N. Wayne
Chicago, IL 60640

Iris, A Journal About Women
The Women's Center
Box 323, HSC
University of Virginia
Charlottesville, VA 22108

Lesbian Connection, For, By & About Lesbians
Helen Diner Memorial Women's Center
Ambitious Amazons
P.O. Box 811
East Lansing, MI 80332

Woman of Power, A magazine of feminism, spirituality, and politics
Woman of Power, Inc.
P.O. Box 2785
Orleans, MA 02653

Books

Adelman, Marcy, Ph.D., *Long Time Passing, Lives of Older Lesbians*, Alyson Publications, Inc., 40 Plympton St., Boston, MA 02118, 1986. (Contains reference list.)

Johnson, Susan E., *Staying Power, Long Term Lesbian Couples*, Naiad Press, Inc., P.O. Box 10543, Tallahassee, FL 32302, 1990 (Contains reference list.)

Sang, Barbara; Warshow, Joyce and Smith, Adrienne J., *Lesbians at Midlife, The Creative Transition*, Spinsters Book Company, P.O. Box 410687, San Francisco, CA 94141, 1991 (Contains reference list.)

 **Mother Courage Press**

In addition to *And Then I Met This Woman, Previously Married Women's Journeys into Lesbian Relationships,* Mother Courage publishes the following titles.

Lesbian

NEWS by Heather Conrad is a gripping novel of a women's computer takeover to make the empire builders and the money makers stop destroying the people and the earth. Paper $9.95

Night Lights by Bonnie Shrewsbury Arthur. More than your traditional lesbian romance, this novel tackles various issues—with a light touch that will make you laugh out loud. Paper $8.95

Singin' the Sun Up by Ocala Wings. Communicating with dolphins gives this lesbian love story a New Age twist. Paper $8.95

Mega by B. L. Holmes. Science fiction lesbian romance set against a future of giant cities and vast pollution of the Earth. Paper $8.95

Hodag Winter by Deborah Wiese. A first grade teacher is fired for being a lesbian. She and her lover and friends fight the action. Paper $8.95

Rowdy & Laughing by B. L. Holmes. She's not gay, she's rowdy and laughing. Poems encompass the joy of life and being in love. Paper $4.95

Senior Citizen by B. L. Holmes. A musical comedy, this funny and touching play explores the dual themes of rejection of the aged, gays and lesbians. Paper $8.95

Self-Help, Sexual Abuse, Prevention

Helping the Adult Survivor of Child Sexual Abuse, for Friends, Family and Lovers by Kathe Stark. Offers guidance for caring support people of a sexual abuse victim to help them with healing while still taking care of themselves. Paper $9.95

Why Me? Help for victims of child sexual abuse, even if they are adults now by Lynn B. Daugherty, Ph.D. Important and informative book for beginning the process of healing the psychological wounds of child sexual abuse. Paper $7.95

Something Happened to Me by Phyllis E. Sweet, M.S. Sensitive, straightforward book designed to help children victimized by sexual or other abuse. Paper $4.95

The Woman Inside, from Incest Victim to Survivor by Patty Derosier Barnes. This workbook is designed to help an incest victim work through pain, confusion and hurt. Paper $11.95

Warning! Dating may be hazardous to your health! by Claudette McShane. Date rape and dating abuse study emphasizes that women need not put up with any kind of abuse, are not to blame for being abused and can regain control of their lives. Paper $9.95

Fear or Freedom, a Woman's Options in Social Survival and Physical Defense by Susan E. Smith. This book realistically offers options to fear of social intimidation and fear of violent crime with an important new approach to self-defense for women. Paper $11.95

I Couldn't Cry When Daddy Died by Iris Galey. Courageous and sensitive personal account of an incest survivor. Story of inspiration and hope. Paper $9.95

Rebirth of Power, Overcoming the Effects of Sexual Abuse through the Experiences of Others, edited by Pamela Portwood, Michele Gorcey and Peggy Sanders, is a powerful and empowering anthology of poetry and prose by survivors of sexual abuse. Paper $9.95

Healing Spells for Sexually Betrayed Women, by Sue Silvermarie. Healing through moving dramatic poetry and through suggestions for visualization and meditation. Paper $8.95

Travel Adventure

Women at the Helm by Jeannine Talley. Two women sell everything and begin an adventure-filled cruise around the world in a 34-foot sailboat. Paper $11.95, Hardcover $19.95

Banshee's Women, Capsized in the Coral Sea by Jeannine Talley. Continuing adventures of Talley and Smith as they are capsized and dismasted off the east coast of Australia. Paper $12.95, Hardcover $21.95

Biography

Olympia Brown, The Battle for Equality by Charlotte Coté. Biography of an unsung foremother, talented orator and the first ordained woman minister in the US who fought a life-long battle for equal rights for women. Paper $9.95, Hardcover $16.95

Humor

Womb with Views, A Contradictionary of the Enguish Language by Kate Musgrave is a delightful, more than occasionally outrageous social commentary cartoon-illustrated feminist dictionary. Paper $8.95

New Age

Welcome to the Home of Your Heart by Dorothy "Mike" Brinkman. Messages of universal love, caring and compassion given to Brinkman by an entity named Jenny. Paper $11.95

Meditations and Blessings from a Different Dimension by Dorothy "Mike" Brinkman. A healing book of channeled meditations and blessings taken from *Welcome to the Home of Your Heart.* Paper $5.95

If you don't find these books in your local book store, you may order them directly from Mother Courage Press at 1533 Illinois Street, Racine, WI 53405. Please add $3 for postage and handling for the first book and 50¢ for each additional book.